Endorsements

Wow! DreamTraders *gives you the tools to move from passion to pursuit! The author's perspective creates content that is applicable at any age. Thought provoking material provides a path to maneuver your "trades" and reach your dreams. Are you ready to step up to the challenge? Buy this book!*

—Stacey South, Community Action Project, Tulsa Director of Admissions & Recruitment

DreamTraders *is for bold thinkers and those looking to do something extraordinary. Heather brilliantly outlines a path for making your dream a reality. A truly unique read that will leave you feeling that anything is possible.*

—Bryan Wilks, Founder of Freeform an Inc 500 Company #2 fastest growing company in Oklahoma, Harvard University, and Stanford Graduate School of Business Alumni

What is deep in Heather's heart, she has successfully put into words that will transform lives—and this, like an arrow will penetrate and motivate hearts. As a teacher, coach, and mentor, Heather has written a detailed plan shining light on the map of success, your success.

So, clear off the table, layout the map of your dreams, and get started on your journey! DreamTraders *will guide, push, encourage, and motivate you every step of the way.*

—Sally Mulready, owner Mulready Properties, CB Select

Heather packs the pages of DreamTraders *with practical ways to bring about self-awareness and then shares the best ways to move forward to your greatest hopes and dreams. She will inspire you to get moving and impact others more than you knew was possible!*

—Tome Dawson, Tulsa Area Pastor, Life.Church

As a Mayor, I can't count the number of times I pitched an idea to the chorus replies of "Dreamer." Dreams are the vision-guides to miracles. DreamTraders brings the understanding and inspiration every dreamer needs to map the miracle path forward.

—Lonnie Sims, City Councilor, former City of Jenks Mayor & State Representative

Heather Turner has written a "How To" manual for getting out of your own way and achieving your dreams. She could have chosen to spend this season of life enjoying the fruits of her labor. Instead, she has generously chronicled and shared her process of creating a beautiful life and successful business. DreamTraders will fan the flames of your passion and move you past dreaming and into action!

—Jenn Milroy, MS, RN, Clinical Instructor, Fran and Earl Ziegler College of Nursing, The University of Oklahoma Health Sciences Center

Wow, what I would have traded to know this wisdom as a young adult. This book serves as a strategic life guide to teach anyone how to turn dreams into reality.

—Meg Weinkauf, MBA, College Professor, Oral Roberts University School of Business, and Founder, The Faithful Leader

I am so proud of Heather Turner. She's committed to following her dreams. But that's not enough. She wants to bring thousands, perhaps millions of dreamers with her to help them see the impossible is possible following God's principles. And that's what good leaders do. DreamTraders is a tribute to life lessons learned—and we are the beneficiaries of her great wisdom.

—Johnie Hampton, CEO, Hampton Creative

Dreams add value to life! Let Heather Turner lead you to discover a pathway for achieving your dreams.

—Stacey Butterfield, Ed.D. Superintendent, Jenks Public Schools

I love Heather's fresh-yet-practical approach to a topic we've all heard before. There's a better way to pursue the life you were meant to live. This enjoyable book will be a valuable help!

—Jeff Anderson, Author of Plastic Donuts and Divine Applause

If there's a dream or vision within you, please don't miss DreamTraders. *Both inspirational and practical, this book is the catalyst you need to not just make your own dream a reality, but also empower those around you to fulfill their greatest calling. Heather Turner is a true advocate and champion for others, and I know you'll love having her in your corner through this book. Grab a copy for yourself and another for a friend!*

—Austin Taylor, Life.Church Online Operations Pastor

Heather is an inspiration to many. She practices what she preaches and has made it her life-long journey to discover and pursue the life she desires. What a gift she has given to all of us with this book—helping us discover who we are and what we will trade so that we also obtain the life we desire. Heather's warmth and love are felt throughout this book as she leads us to think, discover, define, decide, and develop our dreams—guiding us through defeat and detours along the way. Thank you, Heather, for sharing your life experiences as a dream trader.

—Elizabeth Inbody, Executive Director of Jenks Public Schools Foundation

DreamTraders

Discover and Pursue the Life You Want

Heather Turner

Dedication:

DreamTraders is dedicated to my pride and joy, Aidan and Mason Turner. Every word is written with your brightest future in mind. Within each section is a lesson I learned, which I hope will one day help you discover, develop, and duplicate a life full of impact.

With all the trades being made, always know that I wouldn't trade *you,* or the times we have together, for the world.

Love,
Mama

Table of Contents

Foreword

By Mark Roberts, Entrepreneur, business consultant, and Professor of Entrepreneurship at Oklahoma University

This is the story of someone with a dream, a passion, and a family. Someone who wanted to find a way to prioritize her family, and in doing so, created the path to accomplish her dreams. Every dream comes at a cost, and Heather tells a compelling story about how to accomplish your dreams without sacrificing what is most important to you. These pages are filled with life-changing words on how to carefully set your goals to allow you to accomplish the unthinkable. She creates a roadmap to live your dreams.

This book will change the way you live, the way you manage your time, and most importantly, give you the tools you need to succeed in your own journey.

Life will pass you by if you do not have a vision of where you are going. Why waste another breath, when you could live it intentionally?

This book will change your life. After you read it, work it, and live it, get several more copies to give to others you care about.

Introduction:
What Are You Trading?

What would you trade to realize your dream?

My first job, outside of selling cookies or babysitting, was in a telemarketing call center selling caller ID machines. You may be wondering, *What's a caller ID machine?*

Well, youngster, before cell phones were popular and affordable, we didn't have the privilege of knowing who was calling us before we picked up the phone. In 1996, when I turned sixteen years old, caller ID machines were all the rage for your in-home land line.

I had just gotten my drivers license (I probably shouldn't have, looking back at my early driving record), and I needed some cash to pay for 72¢/gallon gasoline and eating out with my friends on the weekends. When I saw that the call center was hiring, and that the only requirements were to be at least sixteen and know how to read, I signed up for an interview! As I recall, it wasn't even a one-on-one interview—it was just a group of people in one room signing documents to begin training. They didn't seem concerned about whether your values aligned with theirs. It was more a question of whether or not you would show up on time to make calls, follow the script, and sell as many caller IDs as possible for $6.50 per hour—plus commissions, if you reached your goals.

I took the job and was supposed to read from a script while making cold calls, offering to sell them this great new device to make their lives easier.

I did well in sales, the only problem was that I didn't stick to the script. I didn't like the spammy feel it gave me, so I figured I could just talk to people like intelligent human beings and let them decide if they wanted to know who was calling or not before they picked up the phone. It turned out that most folks did, and I sold a lot of caller ID machines.

Eventually, I got caught going off script too many times and my boss politely let me go. I had no idea what the mission of the company was (I still don't), but I suppose it was to sell as many devices as possible. I don't remember any talk of core values or a cause worth working toward. It was all about clocking in and making as many calls as you could before clocking out.

For the six months or so that I worked there, I traded my time and ability to read a script to put gas in my car and money in my purse for weekend socializing. It was a means to an end. And I did that job pretty well for a sixteen-year-old…well, until I got canned.

After being let go, I landed a job working for a local bank as a teller. That position did have a one-on-one interview, a background check, a financial check, and more in-depth training to be sure I understood my position and the duties I was expected to perform at a professional level. I really enjoyed meeting people and helping them with their accounts. I learned about banking, customer service, balancing books, and closing out my cash drawer every night. I learned about fraud and having clean books. I learned how to play by the rules as a part of a team. It was a great company to work for and set me up for my next job opportunities. If I'd wanted, I could've stayed there and grown into more opportunities.

I continued working at the bank through my senior year of high school, but being the ambitious girl I am, I took on a second job at JCPenney's photo studio.

I had a friend who worked there and received a great discount on clothing purchases, as JCPenney wanted everyone to look their best on the job. What a cool perk for a seventeen-year-old girl! Plus, it sounded like fun to learn how to take pictures and load film into those huge cameras.

I learned how to "place" families to make everyone look their picture perfect best! If everyone felt their photo was flattering, we'd sell bigger photo packages. I quickly learned what backdrops and lighting worked best for different skin tones. I paid attention to how and where we placed each family member so that each one looked and felt their best.

I enjoyed both sides of photography: the taking of photos and the challenge of selling them. They provided hands-on training and incentives for each level of performance. I really enjoyed working at both the bank and JCPenney for the same reasons: I loved people, teamwork, and individual goal setting, and it felt good to meet customers' needs.

Most of all, I learned about the power of trading.

From Here to There

By the time I finished high school and headed to college, I began to understand the concept of trading time and value in exchange for what was important to me—and had a better understanding of how to best meet the needs of people.

I also began to view work in a different light.

Is work meant to simply be a means to an end? Or can the work, in and of itself, be something of such value that it is the fulfillment of a dream?

Is this type of work meant for a chosen and rare few? Or can we all pursue the work dreams are made of?

This is a topic many have discussed in theory, but we're going to get practical. Today, we dive into:

What in the world are we doing with our dreams?

Where are we headed?

Who are we bringing along for the ride?

The answers to those questions—combined with what it's going to cost—will help us determine whether or not we're willing to make the trades required for our dream to become reality.

DreamTraders

We make trades every day.

Dreams, like anything we want in life, have a cost. We all trade time and money for what we want, so let's approach dreams with the same strategy.

DreamTraders describes the process of Discovering, Defining, Deciding, Developing, Determining the costs, Defeating the odds, handling the Detours, and Duplicating your dreams.

The Duplication of your impact and influence comes when you are not only pursuing your dreams but are also helping others along their dream journeys. As you help others, your impact and influence grows as theirs also grows. Your dream grows beyond self-benefit and acts as a service and inspiration to others.

A DreamTrader is someone who pursues their dreams, is willing to make the trades required to see them fulfilled, and is mindful of helping others do the same. DreamTraders create opportunities and open doors. They are aware of the impact that following their dream can have on the lives of many.

Have you given up on your dreams? Are you tired of fighting for them?

What about trading, instead?

DREAMTRADERS DISCOVER

CHAPTER 1:
Discover Which Type of Trader You Are

You have a dream. And I'd bet you have many. I sure do. The question is, how do we pursue them?

Whether we realize it or not, we go after what we want (or think we want) every day by trading our time, energy, and resources.

Once we consciously embrace the costs and challenges that come along with our dream, we'll carefully identify our motives and who we'll impact should our dreams become reality. With that in mind, we dig into planning our dream path.

When it comes to our dreams, the question isn't "Are we lucky enough?" or "Will we work hard enough?" The core question becomes, "What are we willing to trade for our dream?""

DreamTraders are willing to make two types of trades that others may not be willing to:

1.   Make the trades that cost them whatever it takes to make their dream come true (physical, emotional, time, energy, money, education, to name a few).

2.   Trade their knowledge, care, and influence with others to help them on their dream journey, which creates greater impact.

As with any journey, we can't get to where we're going until we know where we are. To pinpoint where you are in your dream journey, I've identified four trades we most often find ourselves in, either intentionally or by default.

I hope you'll see yourself in one (or all) of the trading types;

TimeTraders:

Most of us begin our working lives this way, trading time for money.

ValueTraders:

People who have something of marketable value that they can trade—and because they understand their worth, they have the option of choosing *who* they trade with.

TalentTraders:

Individuals who have a talent they've developed into a skill that's marketable. This gives them options when it comes to who they work for, *when* they work, and *how* they work.

DreamTraders:

DreamTraders are able to make the trades, sacrifices, and investments needed to go beyond their own dream, which allows them to impact the dreams and destinies of others.

All four Trader types intermingle, but it's up to you which type of Trader you want to be.

If you find yourself in any one of these categories at the moment, know that I'm not saying one type of person is better than another. I've operated in all four categories. What's changed for me is the parameters of what I see as possible, my personal growth in confidence, skill, and leadership, as well as my scope of influence. So in that regard I'm a different person, but the qualities that make me who I am have been the same regardless of which type of trading I've been involved in.

Now that we've named the four main Trader types, let's dig into the details of these trades and find out what type of Trader you are.

The TimeTrader

"Time is Money" pretty much sums up this type of trade.

For a TimeTrader, it's pretty straightforward: they trade their time for dollars. They trade their dollars to meet their needs and maybe even their wants. They may enjoy the folks they work with or may not, but at the end of the day, that's not why they're there.

It's understood that if the money stops, so do they. It's also understood that they'll give a certain number of hours for a certain number of dollars, and that's where the collaborative effort ends. They aren't necessarily employed in their dream job as a TimeTrader, but they are providing for themselves (and/or their family) and that's enough for them. They value the time away from their office more than their time at the office, but they're willing to make that trade because their time at the office makes the time away from it possible to enjoy.

There's no shame in this game. Time trading makes up the majority of jobs around the world. It's what keeps so many important facets of life afloat. The need to provide basic necessities for ourselves and our families is a strong driver, and when needed, just about everyone will trade their time for a dollar every day of the week and twice on Sunday.

Before we feel condemned, or look down our noses at TimeTraders, we need to remember that most of us begin and remain TimeTraders throughout our careers. We should take pride in contributing to our family, and society, by trading time and hard work for dollars.

If you work for a corporation, organization, ministry, school, office, or any other company where your main motivator is money (and you trade hours for it) you are a TimeTrader. Most of us are motivated by money to some degree, so again, that's not a bad thing. We may work for an organization that may not mirror our core values. The work we do may not empower or inspire us toward our hopes and dreams, but it pays the bills.

And to be fair, the values and mission of the company we're employed at may not have been articulated to us. The owners themselves may have lost sight of the reason they started the business. All in all, your purpose for staying in this position is a respectable one. You're providing a living for those you love or for yourself, and that gives you the freedom to do other things you love outside of work. Maybe you play golf or spend time at the gym. Maybe you're a runner, a musician, or an artist who's able to devote weekends and off time to doing what you love because you trade day time for finances to support the life you lead.

Traditionally, we think of work as a means to an end.

If you don't work, you starve, so you work to eat. If you don't work, you don't have a roof over your head or your family's head, so you work to provide shelter. If you don't work, your family goes without the luxuries of modern living like a television or internet access, so you work to provide these things. It's part of what keeps industry, quality of life, and our economy alive.

TimeTraders can make a great living while making a difference in their families and communities by providing a needed good, service, or function. They can build meaningful relationships with their colleagues and do good work together. TimeTraders who are committed to working with integrity will bring excellence and work within the guidelines and expectations set by the companies they work for.

It's where most of us start and most of us stay.

If that's you, keep your chin up and your chest out! You're contributing to family and society, and that's something to take pride in. If you're Time Trading now and have dreams of something more, read on.

You can take the skill and dedication you've developed while trading time and use it to launch into Value Trading.

I'm a TimeTrader Checklist:

❏   I'm not sure what the core values of the organization I work for are, or maybe I know them but don't necessarily align with them.

❏   My main motivation for staying in my current position is financial security. Even if I'm not rollin' in the dough, at least I have some dough to roll.

❏   I'm able to provide for my needs and/or the needs of my family trading my time for money. I find great value in that, as do the family members I support.

❏   I didn't necessarily set out to do what I do for a living, but it's a skill I learned and now it would be hard to start over in a new industry.

❏   I sometimes think about what it would be like to do something I truly loved for a living.

Talk, Trade, and Takeaway:

1. If you identify as a TimeTrader, what do you feel is your greatest motivator for staying in your current position?

_____

_____

_____

2. Since time is money, do you feel you're currently getting a fair trade? Does the time you invest give you the monetary return you feel your time is worth?

_____

_____

_____

3. In defining TimeTraders, we mentioned that the company or organization you work for may or may not have the same core

values you do. What are *your* top five core values? This knowledge will help you as we move forward to other types of trade.

_____

_____

_____

_____

ValueTraders

What do you value in life? What's important to you every single day? And what values are you willing to work toward?

Value traders are dedicated to finding a career in a field they truly enjoy, while working to contribute something of real value. This type of position meets not only the physical needs of the employee with financial reward (still trading hours for dollars), but they are also gaining experience in a field they're passionate about—or at least feel is one that is valuable and worthy of what they can bring to the table.

Their core values and ethics align with that of the organization for the most part and they feel they are doing work with purpose.

ValueTraders have a lot going for them. They have managed to find the perfect combination of trading time for dollars with a company or organization that contributes to their overall career choice satisfaction.

Here are some factors to consider when determining if you are a TimeTrader or ValueTrader.

I am a ValueTrader Checklist:

❑   My Core Values: Align with that of the organization who employs me.

❑   My Financial Needs are met: Salary is competitive and shows that the organization values what I bring to the table. I would love to make more of course, but I feel fairly compensated.

❑   Meets "I'm doing work that matters" emotional need: I feel I am doing work that is valuable and rewarding. My work not only meets my financial needs, but also gives me a sense of purpose. I am bringing, and trading, valuable skills, knowledge, ideas, and productivity within an organization that is making a positive impact on the community or beyond. (Think of teachers, nurses, doctors, nonprofit workers, medical staff, and the list goes on.) When you are working for any organization or company that has a cause you can get behind, it brings immense value to your work life.

❑   I have Future Opportunity: As a ValueTrader who works in a strong organization, I can see future opportunity within the organization itself, or opportunity within the job market at large if I perform well within my current organization. I have hope for more opportunity ahead, and that's a very important part of job contentment.

❑   I have Opportunity for Continued Development: As a ValueTrader, I enjoy having a position that offers me growth and developmental opportunities at the company's expense. Whether it's education or mentorship, this is a great benefit that many companies offer to further the potential growth of their employees.

❑   I receive Benefits: I receive family medical and dental benefits. I receive other intangible benefits of the rewarding work I do. It's a big part of my decision-making process in choosing my career. (Benefits are always something to consider when taking on a new position or choosing to go out on your own as an entrepreneur. Medical and Dental insurance coverage can be very costly and having a portion paid by your employer makes a difference. Vacation time away from the daily work routine is also an important part of staying emotionally and physically healthy. Companies who approve time away and paid vacation time are sought after by ValueTraders.)

It's a wonderful thing to work within an organization that not only values what you have to offer, but also provides a place where you can grow in your career.

Value in the Future

If a company can offer upward movement, a cause you can get behind, core values and a mission that align with your own, with the added bonus of medical and dental benefits so your kiddos can get those braces— wow, that's a great place to build a career! ValueTraders are happy to trade their talent, skills, and time to add value to an organization. It's a fair trade that serves both sides well.

When I graduated college in December of 2003 with a degree in music education, there weren't any music teaching positions available at our local public schools. My graduation landed in the middle of the fiscal school year and as a newlywed on a tight budget, it was time to go job hunting.

Before graduating, I was student teaching in the day time and working at a bank call center in the evenings. I also had a job teaching a few music classes and lessons with a small music school. I loved teaching and my newly-earned degree made it the perfect place to gain experience, and help make ends meet until the schools posted open positions for the next fall.

I ran all over town teaching music classes during the day and working the call center at night. It just wasn't the best use of my time or in our best interest financially. Once we tired of Ramen noodles and boxed mac n cheese, I applied and accepted a position at a local law firm editing petitions for homes and land plats for a title company. It was a reputable firm and I was grateful for the work. My salary was $28,000 per year and I thought I hit the big time. I love people, so that part of the job was easy. However, being stuck inside a cubicle most of the day was like torture. For eight months I worked in that cubicle and watched the clock slowly tick the days away.

The position lacked creativity and face-to-face interaction. When July rolled around, a nearby public school system posted an opening for a full-time music teacher. To say I jumped on that opportunity with enthusiasm is an understatement. I landed the job! It was time to put my education, passion for music and love for people into action, and I couldn't wait for the first day of class!

I was responsible for general music education instruction for grades first through fourth, as well as middle school and high school vocal music. I loved planning lessons and sharing about the different genres and composers of music. It was fun making up games to teach notation, and putting on musicals. Although some days were challenging and I was working more hours than I ever had before, the work was fulfilling. In the three years I taught at Mounds Public schools I learned a great deal about classroom management, scope and sequence in setting goals for progress, parent and family interaction, and conflict resolution. I learned how to fundraise and budget for supplies. We put on shows and traveled together for special performances.

Over those years I began to gain a deeper understanding of the purpose I was to fulfill in teaching music. It became more than notes on a page or songs to sing. It was work worthy of bringing my best—because when I did, it mattered. It gave opportunity and expanded horizons for students. The core values of the school system were clear and aligned with my own.

With rewarding work, aligned values, financial benefit, and experience with room to grow, I transitioned from a TimeTrader to a ValueTrader. It wasn't an overnight transition. In fact, I thought I brought more value than I probably did—right out of college with my head full of musical terminology and instructional methods. It took time for my side of the value trade to balance out with the value I was receiving in that position.

When it came time to move on, I had a truer perspective and a little more to bring to the table. I taught four more years in both public and private school systems—both choices in an effort to do what was best for our growing family.

It was in those years of Value Trading that I gained a love for education and a passion for finding potential (sometimes hidden) in people and drawing it out. It's what prepared me for what I do today. Value trading was a foundational building block for my career and I wouldn't trade that for the world. Honestly, I could have stayed a ValueTrader in public education for my entire career. That would have been a very rewarding and meaningful legacy to leave.

If you are lucky enough to be a ValueTrader at a great organization, count yourself blessed. Value trading is a great place to build a life and legacy—but it's not the only worthy trade to make.

Talk, Trade, and Takeaway:

1. If you identify as a ValueTrader, what do you feel the organization brings to the community, and its staff, to add value?

   _____

   _____

   _____

   _____

2. What value are *you* trading in return?

   _____

   _____

   _____

   _____

3. In planning for the future, what opportunities lie ahead for you within or outside of your current organization?

   _____

   _____

   _____

   _____

Action Step:

1. Look for small ways to add *extra* value to your position at the organization. Serve others beyond what is expected! Write down two new ways you can serve this week.

   _____

   _____

   _____

   _____

The TalentTrader

Often defined as the risk-taker or entrepreneur who knows what they are passionate about, TalentTraders choose freedom over stability, although many have both.

They are willing to work without many of the usual benefits and opportunities a structured organization can offer, in favor of the freedom that going it on their own allows them. Not to say they wouldn't appreciate things like health-care and sick-leave, but when the choice is freedom or structure, they'll choose freedom every time.

Think about your hair stylist, the mechanic who fixes your car, the health or beauty consultant next door, or the lady who keeps your nails looking perfect. From doctors, lawyers, business consultants, and web designers, to artists and guitar instructors, there are millions of TalentTraders who trade their talent and skill for dollars.

They may do it for a company or freelance. They may open their own shop or work from their homes, but they have one thing in common. They have a tradable talent or skill that others value enough to pay them for, and they have found a way to make a living out of it on their own terms.

TalentTraders take pride in the skills they've developed, and for good reason. They have invested the time, taken the classes, paid their dues, to grow a client base and reputation based upon their recognized talent.

TalentTraders are often able to make a great living working for themselves. They are able to guarantee a quality service or product with the knowledge that they will do what it takes to please the customer.

Great organizations seek TalentTraders as employees for a variety of reasons, but most importantly, they bring in business. Their talent for their craft, sport, art, trade, or interpersonal skills is noticeable and valuable.

TalentTraders can work within an organization but they like to play by their own rules.

They seek out creative ways to bring results and can feel stifled by too many rules and restrictions. TalentTraders know where they shine and are confident enough to do it on their own. They can build a clientele. And even though they may lack strong time management skills, their reputation for quality results gets them opportunity after opportunity.

My Parable of Talents

My college years were immersed in music from morning to night. When I wasn't in class or university rehearsal, I was at church leading worship or teaching parts at choir rehearsal, or doing my best to learn the piano part for the weekend worship set.

These were key developmental years—full of small triumphs and failures, I learned how to better lead and follow. After several years developing in our small town church, my husband Jon and I got the request to help launch a new campus of Life.Church (then LifeChurch.tv). Their newly hired worship pastor called and set up a meeting with Jon and my brother-in-law, Tom.

Even though we weren't sure what all we were in for, we felt it was the right thing at the right time, so with youthful boldness, we said "yes!"

Then, I cried.

Launching a new church campus meant leaving the comfort and familiarity of the church where we were married, began our life and ministry together, and fostered wonderful relationships. Our longtime church home gave us our start in ministry as a couple and it's always hard to leave what you know to venture into the unknown.

But it was time. We both knew it. Time to take on the next season of life together with an incredible organization. It was the most beautiful combination of value and talent trading. Don't get me wrong, our talent was not all that impressive. We needed more development, but how better to grow than to be challenged and stretched out of our comfort zones?

Life.Church valued excellence and backed that belief up by compensating their worship bands as contractors. We had never been compensated for preparing and leading worship before. It was the first time we became TalentTraders for a calling we would follow—with or without compensation.

Maybe that's how you know it's your passion and heart. Maybe your talent and passion collide in a trade that acknowledges that the skill you bring is worthy of compensation.

Sometimes talent trading and Value Trading don't go hand in hand, but when they do it's a remarkable privilege. Once you have developed a skill that the market deems valuable, something pretty cool can happen—you get to be a little more selective about which companies, organizations, or causes you partner with. That's one of the best parts about talent trading.

When you start out developing a talent or skill, you must take whatever work you can get. You can't demand your price before you have earned a reputation for excellence; the market gets to determine value. But as your talent or skill grows and you build a reputation for bringing excellence, you will get to choose *who* you trade your talent with.

And that's a beautiful thing.

Many folks combine talent and Value Trading for the perfect cocktail of careers, and enjoy both value and creative freedoms. If you're thinking of talent trading on your own terms, here are a few things to consider to see if you're up for the challenge. Read below to see if you fit the TalentTrader description on it's own and *not* paired with another Trader type—as it pertains to going out on your own, outside of any organizational structure to rely on.

TalentTraders Need a Few Things to Stay in the Game:

❏   Creative Control: I'm not happy in someone else's box, it feels too tight in there and I want to rearrange the furniture! I prefer to create my own methods over following someone else's protocol. Although I'm willing to play with a team or within professional parameters of an organization, I like to have some room to experiment and find out what environment lends itself to bringing out my best.

❏   I want the freedom to choose my own schedule or at least have flexibility to dictate my schedule.

❏   Sure I like praise, but competition and naysayers also fuel me. Cheer me on. Great. But tell me I can't and I'll show you I can!

❏   I need some financial return. It's not my driving force, because I can't help but do what I love, but if I don't get paid, my spouse/partner is gonna put the kibosh on this gig. Compensation is also one way I can measure my value and skill level.

❏   I want the freedom and hope of a greater future. I like the idea that my future is as bright as the work and skill I bring to the table. I understand I am only limited by myself and that excites me about what is possible.

Talk, Trade, and Takeaway:

1. What talent or skill do you need to develop in order for the market to trade dollars for it?

   _____

   _____

   _____

   _____

2. What talent or skill are you already trading that you can take to the next level?

_____

_____

_____

_____

3. On the list of things needed for TalentTraders to stay in the game, did any not apply for you? Why?

_____

_____

_____

_____

Action Steps:

1. If you have talent in an area, but know that without development you won't get the opportunity to make a trade for financial gain, write that area down.

_____

_____

_____

_____

2. Now write your most logical *next step* for development in that area? Lessons, classes, internship, small opportunity to gain experience, etc.

_____

_____

_____

_____

The DreamTrader: Where Value, Talent, and Cause Collide.

The person who is able to make the necessary trades, and sacrifices, for their dreams—while simultaneously bringing other dreamers alongside to for influence and impact—is a DreamTrader.

One dreamer living out her dream can make a difference. But when you build a team of dreamers their strengths, dreams, influence, and opportunity collide, multiplying their impact.

Ecclesiastes 4:9 says, "Two are better than one because they have a good return on their labor." DreamTraders understand that there is power in numbers. They know that being vigilant in pursuit of their dreams, as well as contributing to the dream journeys of those around them, will serve to multiply their own strength, influence, effectiveness, and opportunity. They aren't helping others with selfish motives or thoughts of "I'll scratch your back if you scratch mine." They simply understand that life is more fulfilling when you live it in service of others.

Serving builds relationship, relationship builds trust, trust builds influence, influence opens door to greater impact.

Now that you know my working definition of a DreamTrader is twofold, (making the trades necessary to pursue your dream *and* bringing others alongside to help them accomplish their dreams) let's look at the DreamTraders checklist.

DreamTraders Checklist:

❑   I'm living out my dream with a constant awareness of how I can bring others alongside in a mutually beneficial effort.

❑   I trade my time, talent, and skill to bring value to an organization with whom I share core values and am aligned with in mission. Or…

❑   I trade my time, talent, and skill to bring value to an organization I founded.

❑   I intentionally pursue growth in education and opportunity for myself *and* those around me.

❑   I understand that when I learn, I have more to offer others. I understand that when I help others grow in opportunity, I get to be a small part of their successes.

❑   I'm willing to answer the tough questions, make the hard choices, and pay the price to live out my dream. I'm aware that it won't always be cupcakes and puppies, but it'll be worth it.

Are you ready to be a DreamTrader?

CHAPTER 2:

Discover Your DreamTrader Journey

Our journey together will follow this path:

Discover:

We began with discovering the four types of trade: Time Trading, Value Trading, Talent Trading, and Dream Trading. These trading types can stand on their own or be combined. Now, we will get personal and discover more about your strengths, history—and of course, your dreams.

Define:

Once you know where you are in the trade game, you'll be able to set goals for where you want to go. We all have aspirations to reach a dream and lead a life of significance. We fiercely determine to forge ahead as we continue to dive deeper into who we are and where we're headed.

Decide:

At this point in our journey, we are making active decisions. To be successful, it's important to take inventory and make smart decisions about how to use fear to fuel you, take charge of your self-talk, and learn to prioritize your priorities.

Don't:

Just as sure as there are important things to do toward seeing your dreams fulfilled, there are things DreamTraders don't do. Later, I'll share four traps to avoid.

Develop:

The path from where we are to where dreams start to become reality is paved with costs, challenges, realizations of self and surroundings, and decisions about who should (or shouldn't) be a travel companion. Together we'll develop a plan for your success, with solutions for how to handle twists and turns on our journey.

Determine:

Now that we have defined your dream and developed a plan of action toward its success, we dive deeper to determine the true costs of your dream. This a vital step for DreamTraders, as it will determine whether or not you are headed in the right direction. If making these determinations enlightens you to change your path (because the trades required are too costly) this is the time to make those determinations and gain clarity.

You can't determine costs or trades required for anything until you know what you desire. That's why this section has to come *after* you define your dream and have a plan of how to arrive there.

Defeat:

At this point in your journey you've defined your dream, developed a plan, determined the costs and trades required, and are making headway! This section gives you the tools you need to defeat the obstacles that are sure to pop up along dream journey. Together we learn how to defeat conformity and distraction. When we begin to feel overwhelmed—or find ourselves exhausted or losing focus on our journey—we take a pit stop to refresh ourselves and get back on the road.

Detour:

After embracing the fact that the journey won't be a straight, smooth line, we understand that we'll face interruptions and collisions. With even greater tenacity, we choose to continue on our journey. We learn how to see detours as possible onramps to opportunity. We get super practical with methods to use to embrace change. We learn that mapping and planning is vital to ending up someplace *intentionally*—rather than simply ending up someplace.

Duplicate:

Lastly, we celebrate the slow evolution we experience as we morph from who we once were into a clearer picture of who we hope to become. As our perspective of what's possible changes, so does our capacity to look outside our own interests—to see the needs, goals, and dreams of others. When we're no longer in survival mode, we can help others on their journey and celebrate with them as they make strides toward their dreams.

Discover What Type of Dreamer You Are

We are all dreamers, but if you aren't sure you how to define what that looks and feels like for you, let's start there.

Some folks get dreams and goals confused. For our purposes we will define dreams as your big picture of hope. It's the experience of who and what you hope to become—and who and what you want to be around you.

When people say "I'm livin' the Dream," they're talking about experiencing a reality of what they hoped for. This includes family, career, relationships, faith, health, security, freedom, independence, influence, or significance—whatever the components are for you.

Goals on the other hand are the planning of, preparing for, and execution of action steps toward making your dreams reality. Action steps toward those goals put hope into motion and create momentum toward your dream.

Dreams are the big picture of hope.

Goals are the thoughtful plans to reach those hopes.

Action steps toward those goals are the workings of what makes your dream reality.

As the saying goes, "It's simple, but not easy." I used to think maybe some folks just didn't have a dream. Now I know everyone has a dream, great or small, but realizing it means owning it. Being responsible for our dreams means being vulnerable to the pain of failure or rejection.

Dreams can be scary to share because of the responsibility that comes with them. Let's discover together what type of dreamer you are.

The Passionate Dreamer

"I can't stop thinking about this. I can't ignore it. I can't put it out of my mind or replace it. I can't pretend it doesn't matter. I have to go after this passion, this idea, this burning inside that tells me there's something I'm meant to be and do!"

Does this sound like you?

It's an unction, a desire, a fire, a deeply felt belief or calling you can't always explain—but it's always there.

But to put your dream into words would make it real, and that's a bit scary, maybe even intimidating. You fear it sounds too big, audacious, or even prideful to put breath behind it. *Have you gotten too big for your britches?* You wonder, but you write it down privately, just to see how the dream looks on paper.

You pray for it. Even that feels a bit self-serving because there are so many others in need of more attainable things. Why not just pray for the masses to be fed or world peace, but not your own burning purpose.

But wait. Is it possible that your own purpose—that prayer answered—could have an incredible, even life-changing effect on the masses if it were to be fulfilled?

If you don't say it aloud, write it down, view it, envision it, pray for wisdom to pursue it, and take action, your dream might not become reality—in your life and in the lives of others.

It's just as dangerous to neglect a calling as it is scary to pursue one.

There's no guarantee that what you had in mind, even thoughtfully planned and executed, will have the final result you expected. There's simply more in the works than what we can see or predict. And that's the collision of excitement and risk. It's what multiplies the ripple effect of millions of people pursuing their dreams. It's the knowledge, without any tangible evidence, that you have something. Something meant to share.

There's not an arrogance in this journey. It is not a condescending view of average or normal, it's simply your truth.

If that's you, if you can't free your thoughts from the calling upon you, you are my definition of a Passionate Dreamer.

The Practical Dreamer

You want a life that has meaning and impact. But others may not see your dream as anything fancy or audacious.

What is important isn't what others perceive to be significant or fancy. Own your dream. Don't get caught up in comparing your dream to someone else's.

Maybe you'd like to own a small business or write a book. Your dream could be raising your children to be strong leaders and creating nutritious meals for your family. You may dream of living in a sleepy beach town or a bustling city. Your hope may be to provide a comfortable living for your family while giving generously to your community and beyond.

What some may see as "practical," others experience as a dream come true.

Talk, Trade, and Takeaway:

1. Do you see yourself as a more passionate or more practical dreamer?

   _____

   _____

   _____

   _____

2. Do you worry about what others might think, or say, if you shared your dream?

   _____

   _____

   _____

   _____

Discover Your Beginnings

Remember when you were eight years old, with your whole life ahead of you, and your second-grade teacher asked, "What do you want to be when you grow up?" What was your answer?

I'm pretty sure I wanted to be a veterinarian. I loved dogs so much, and constantly brought home the free pups that people gave away at the local Walmart parking lot.

That dream was tied for first place with a desire to be a famous singer. I have loved to sing for as long as I can remember. I didn't think of the schooling, preparation, dedication, or commitment that would be required for either of those dreams to become reality. I didn't know what the day to day work habits looked like for either of those career paths, I just thought they sounded like a lot of fun. Endless puppies and stardom couldn't be all that bad right?

Youth is fueled with the expectation of endless possibility. That hope, the innocent expectation of greatness, is a true gift to all of us. It's in that hope that we find the determination to propel us onward toward our dream. When we are just starting out, it's easy to pronounce a dream without knowledge of the skill, sacrifice, and dedication it will take to make that dream a reality. In many cases, it's youth's advantage.

Sometimes youthful boldness and confidence is exactly the launching pad we need.

However, as we "grow up" most of us let our fears—and the possibility of rejection or failure—silence the big dreams we once had. We trade big dreams for what seems more reachable, practical, and sustainable. That's not to say practicality is a bad thing or that practical dreamers who make dreams a reality can't sustain them, but the bumps and bruises of life often try to convince us that the cost of a great dream is too great. We aren't always so sure we have what it takes to fit the bill. Sometimes we simply aren't willing to pay the price.

Maybe the price to be a rock star is to live in your car and play back-to-back shows for next to nothing for years on end before you get your "big break." Everyone isn't cut out for that.

Maybe you've got to trade security and family time in order to chase that dream, with no guarantee for the pot of gold at the end of the rainbow. Maybe the price to be the top surgeon in the country is dedicating the first twenty-five years of your career to experimental research and innovative—even risky—surgical methods that other surgeons may question.

Big dreams most often have a big price tag. As hard as it is to hear, in most cases, you get what you pay for—or get what you *trade* for.

Talk, Trade, and Takeaway:

1. How did you answer the "What do you wanna be when you grow up?" question as a child?

    _____

    _____

    _____

    _____

2. Did you become that? If so, did it happen the way you planned and look how you thought it would?

    _____

    _____

    _____

    _____

3. Do you agree with "You get what you trade for" in life or do you live more by the "When my ship comes in..." philosophy?

    _____

    _____

    _____

    _____

Discover Your True Identity

How can I see myself for all I can be, instead of defining who I am by where I am?

My first teaching position was at a rural school of about 1,000 students. I taught first through twelfth-grade music. The school was labeled "Title One" as it served a high percentage of students who were economically underprivileged. I remember asking my students what they wanted to do when they graduated.

The first and second-graders usually had the typical answers: they'd enthusiastically reply with their choice to be a doctor, a teacher, or a fireman—or a veterinarian who was a rock star on the weekends.

But when I asked my high school students the same question, the response was quite different. Many of my high school girls would say, "I wanna get married and have kids." The boys might reply with, "I don't know, maybe get a job."

Marriage, children, and steady work are admirable goals to strive toward, but I couldn't help but wonder what their childhood dreams had once been. It made me sad to realize the limits of what they saw as possible for themselves.

I suspect some of these students once had dreams of being the first in their family to graduate high school and go to college. Maybe they wanted to be the first to own a home or be a teacher, doctor, or business owner. I wondered what changed between age eight and eighteen? What circumstance had blinded their mind's eye to the possibilities?

When they saw poverty, neglect, and hunger on a daily basis, maybe getting married and having a child that both parents raised together was a big dream. If your parents never held a steady job or earned enough income to support their family without government assistance, a steady job with benefits would feel like living the dream.

No matter how big their dreams, I remember wanting to open each student's eyes to bigger possibilities—not in an effort to entice them with materialistic goals, but to show them that they were not limited to the quality of life they'd grown accustomed to.

There's a saying in education, "Students who are hungry, come to school for food and love. Students who are well loved and fed at home, come to school to learn." Hopefully we are educating all students, but the truth is that when they're concerned about their next meal, a safe place to sleep at night, or having clean clothing to wear, multiplication tables and correct grammar just aren't high on their priority list.

And the same is true for adults. It's hard to think about big, exciting dreams when you're in survival mode.

Are you struggling to dream bigger because you don't believe you can experience anything better than what you've been surrounded by your whole life? Do you feel stuck in survival mode and want out but aren't sure how?

Maybe you aren't in economic hardship, but you might be focused on your relationships surviving. Perhaps you struggle with insecurity, depression, or anxiety and it takes every ounce of courage to get out of bed each morning and go through the necessary tasks of the day. You may have lost a loved one unexpectedly and you're just not sure where to go from here. Maybe you had a scary health report that has overwhelmed your thoughts and kept you from hoping for a brighter future. You may feel that the work you do is getting overlooked and the effort you put in seems to be in vain, and that has deflated your spirits.

Whatever it is that has you in survival mode, let me share a few things I remind myself of when I'm going through hard times.

1. I'm still alive, so my story isn't finished yet. I can choose to let the circumstances of life write my story or I can get myself up, wipe away my tears, and start the work of writing my own story. *I didn't get to choose where or how I started out, but I do get to choose how I approach the finish line.*

2. God's word says He will never leave me or forsake me, I'm not alone, even when I feel lonely.

3. God's word says He has good plans for my life; plans for me to prosper.

4. I can be a victim or a victor, but not both at the same time. I get to choose who I want to be.

5. I will reap what I sow. I will ultimately receive what I give. I can make the most of a situation and learn from it, or I can complain to no avail. The choice is up to me.

6. I am responsible for my own pursuit of happiness, wholeness, and success. It's not anyone else's job to make me happy, whole, or successful.

Talk, Trade, and Takeaway:

1. What do you think changed between elementary school and high school that had such an impact on the way the students answered the question, "What do you want to be when you grow up?"

   _____

   _____

   _____

   _____

2. What labels or limitations have you allowed to change the way you identify yourself?

   _____

   _____

   _____

   _____

3. List three true, positive qualities that are traits of your true identity.

   _____

   _____,_____

   _____

   _____

Discover Your Strengths

What makes you, you? If I were to ask your friends and family to use five words that best describe you, what would those five words be?

Funny, Friendly, Shy, Loud, Secretive, Smart, Thoughtful, Inquiring, Adventurous, Musical, Daring, Reflective, Cautious, Bold, Kind, Athletic, Artistic, Creative, Quiet.

These are just a few words that you or others may use to describe your strengths or personality traits. Maybe you're really good at cultivating relationships or developing teams. Maybe you're a creative who can take small resources and create big results. Maybe you're the one people come to with their problems, knowing you'll help find solutions. Maybe you prefer time with a computer and analytics over time with people. That's okay. This section of discovery is all about discovering your *strengths*.

What seems to come pretty naturally to you that others may have to work harder to succeed at? Are you a good, patient listener? That's a valuable strength that many of us wish we had. Are you great at talking to new people without feeling self-conscious? Let's get to know you a little better. Complete the Talk, Trade, and Takeaway section below.

Talk, Trade, and Takeaway:

1. What five words would your closest friends and family use to describe you?

   _____

   _____

   _____

   _____

2. If you had an entire day to do whatever you wanted, what would you choose to do?

   _____

   _____

   _____

   _____

3. What is something you try to avoid at all costs?

   _____

   _____

   _____

   _____

4. List your top five strengths below.

   _____

   _____

   _____

   _____

CHAPTER 3:
Define Your Fears and Trade them for Faith

The household I grew up in was a whole, loving one, with too many good memories to count, but there was more to the story than what met the eye.

The church we attended faithfully had a very strong influence in our lives—both good and bad. If I had to guess, I would say most of our lives are blessed with this mixture. It was easy to see the good in the close friendships we shared, the safe and happy home environment we enjoyed, and the relationship we developed with Christ. Unfortunately, the bad did place a filter on a big portion of our lives growing up. Fear was the chosen tool, used often by our spiritual leaders to manipulate the congregants of the church.

Fear of losing salvation. Fear of displeasing God. Fear of not measuring up. Fear of rejection. Fear of being disapproved of by people in general. Fear of sin. Fear of failure. Fear of being influenced by people outside of our safety net. Fear of the unknown. Lots and lots of fear!

It seemed I was constantly striving to gain the approval of my pastor or other spiritual leaders (which they equated with God's approval) and I constantly came up short.

I didn't know all I was capable of, but I knew God created me with purpose and with a heart for people. I sought approval and acceptance for too many years and was left wanting. When it was time for me to move away for college, I was able to leave the legalistic church environment that had become so oppressive. But overcoming the many forms of fear that had become a constant in my life, didn't happen overnight. It took years of learning about breaking "approval addiction" and receiving God's grace, before I understood and embraced the fact that I was already approved.

I didn't have to *earn* God's approval and I didn't have to live in fear of constantly missing the mark. I could live in the approval He had already given when He gave His son Jesus for me. My works, my "striving to be holy," would not make His love for me any greater. That truth was, and still is, huge for me.

Once I embraced this truth, a whole new world opened up for me to explore. Of course, I still had to work very hard for every step toward my dream, but I was no longer held back by the fear of someone else's disapproval. As I took steps to overcome my approval addiction, I also took steps to see past other hurdles like the lack of finances, and not knowing the "right people" to open doors.

It's pretty cool how trading one bad filter (fear) for a good one (faith) brightens up your entire life.

The trading part is vital. It's one thing to know what you're afraid of but another thing entirely, to replace your fear with faith. Once you begin to make that trade actively, it will change your life—just like it did mine.

So, here goes your first, vitally important trade. Let's do it together.

Let everything else in your world go quiet for a few moments. Let your deepest fears reveal themselves. And face them. Name them.

Now it's time to make what may be the most important trade on your dream journey, let's trade fear for faith!

Fears you'll have to Trade for Faith:

Fear:	Faith:
Fear of hurting someone's feelings by going somewhere new.	I will be better equipped to help you if I help myself. I have to choose me.
Fear of Unknown.	I trust that with God's help, and my hard work, my future will be better than I imagined.
Fear of Failure.	I choose to learn from every success and every failure. Failing is an event not a person. When I fail I know that doesn't make me a failure.
Fear of being found wanting.	We all have areas of lack. Finding out where those are for me will only help me grow and surround myself with people who have strength in that area.
Fear of letting someone down.	It's bound to happen. I commit to building far more people up than I ever let down.
Fear of Rejection.	Jesus and Steve Jobs were rejected. That's a weird pairing but great compahy! We don't live for the approval of people but out of the approval of the God who created us.
Fear of	
Fear of	
Fear of	

CHAPTER 4:
Define Proximity as a Good Teacher

It was late March of 1999 when the phone finally rang. That day would change my path.

I answered the phone to hear Professor Goldman-Moore on the phone. "We'd like to offer you a scholarship for Vocal Performance at the University of Tulsa. Would you like to accept?"

I was instantly thrilled and surprised. "Yes!"

My dream of being a professional singer—maybe even a star—had just begun! I enrolled in the University of Tulsa as a Vocal Performance Major. I loved to sing, I loved the stage, and although my opportunities had been limited, I had big dreams!

By the end of my freshman year I auditioned and was added to the cast of three light operas for Light Opera Oklahoma. It was an exciting time of growth. The entire summer was a blur of long rehearsals until finally it was showtime.

We had a great cast with the best leads and choreographers. I was the new kid and just happy to be in the chorus or dance line. As I got to know the actresses, actors, singers, and dancers I learned that most had one thing in common. They were employed only until the show was over, and then they would go audition in whatever city they could get work. It was an adventurous lifestyle.

These were highly-talented creatives who lived for the arts. They gave their life to it. Many hoped to go to Broadway, and the opera's leads were from New York. It was in meeting these artists who were sold out to their music careers that I realized I wasn't willing to make the trades to be a Broadway star.

I loved singing, enjoyed being on the stage, had a great connection with the other members of the cast—and knew if I worked hard I could go far. But all that didn't matter because through the experience I discovered this wasn't my true passion.

I wasn't up at night thinking of ways I could improve on the stage. I wasn't desperate for the next role or solo, I wasn't willing to pay the price for what I thought was my big dream. That's how I knew it wasn't my destiny. Proximity had been a very good teacher.

Showbiz wasn't my true path. It was time to re-evaluate and find out what was. It was time to embrace change and trade what I thought my dream was for something new.

I cried over my loss. It felt like I was giving up. What I know now is that my dream was being tested. I still knew I loved music and I loved to sing. I knew I had a gift for relating with people. Because I love people, it's really easy for me to connect in a genuine way with almost anyone.

Hmm… Music. And people.

I cared greatly about seeking out the potential in others and helping them develop it. (Perhaps this was birthed from the hope that someone would do this for me.) I had an amazing voice instructor who did, Karen Smith-Pearson. She saw in me what I couldn't see in myself and she opened the door of opportunity for college that I wouldn't have approached in the same light.

I wanted to do the same for others. I wanted to teach. I traded the dream of being on stage in musicals, for the dream of inspiring others through music from a classroom instead of a stage. Of course as it worked out, I'm still able to enjoy stage time, but not at the same trade rate as required by doing it as a full-time career.

I changed my major to music education with an emphasis on Vocal Performance. This would afford me the opportunity to teach and put to use the vocal pedagogy and general music education I had earned. I graduated 2003 with a Bachelors of Music Education and started teaching Music and Choral Music the Fall after graduation.

My former dream had changed, but my true purpose had evolved from it. I was willing to pay the price for this one. It would mean early mornings and late days after school. It would mean raising money for instruments and musicals, and making costumes out of sheets. It would mean learning to teach from where students were able to learn, not reeling off pedagogical methods I learned in college that they couldn't yet understand. It meant humility. It meant putting students first. It meant learning to look at education through a parent's eyes.

It meant growing up, and I loved every minute of it.

Dreams grow. And when we follow our dreams, we'll grow, too.

Talk, Trade, and Takeaway:

1. Earlier in the book you wrote down your childhood dream. Has your dream stayed the same or has it evolved and grown into something else?

   _____

   _____

   _____

   _____

2. Evolving and growing dreams can feel similar to letting go of dreams. How can you determine the difference between evolving into a different, greater version of your dream and giving up on your former dream?

   _____

   _____

   _____

   _____

3. Do you think it's okay to ever give up on a dream? If so why?

   _____

   _____

   _____

   _____

How Can You Embrace Proximity?

When you can get close to what you think you want to *do*, or *who* you think has something you'd like to have, spend some time with them. See how they spend their days and weekends. See how much time they have for family, friends, faith, entertainment, or relaxation. There's almost always a gap between how we *think* our dream life will play out and what living the dream really looks like.

I call it the 90-10 principle. The 90-10 principle is one based on the 10% stage time or the "cool" part everyone sees, versus the much larger 90% time you work to prepare for what everyone else sees. You can take most careers and see how this plays out. Use our business, a music school, for example.

The 10% which people see includes: fun, concerts, community showcases, rockstar teaching teams, and music filled studios with happy students entering and exiting with guitars, violins, and brass instruments.

The 90% it took—and still takes—to get to all the fun stuff was four and a half years in college, seven and a half years teaching public school music, ten years or more of leading worship at church, lesson planning, building relationships, learning how to communicate effectively with parents, approaching different learning styles, taking risks like leaving tenured teaching positions, trading savings to open the studio, recruiting people (with high character, high talent, and a love for people), training and developing them, paying them, (and overhead costs—before paying myself), taking responsibility for losses, advertising, cleaning toilets, taking out trash, refilling paper-towel and toilet paper holders, bill collecting, schedule sorting, lease negotiating, and the list goes on!

The same goes for any occupation. The NFL player spends 90% (or more) of their time preparing. The pastor spends 90% of time preparing, praying, visiting the sick, marrying and burying folks, strategic planning, writing, and counseling—and about 10% (or less) of the time teaching from stage.

If you never get in proximity to see the 90% of whatever industry you are interested in pursuing, you may be chasing the elusive—and sometimes deceptive—10%.

Now, don't get me wrong, if it's *your* dream to catch, it's worth the time spent cleaning toilets or negotiating lease agreements. Just remember that is part of the trade that has to be made to see dreams become reality. It's worth the late nights, burst waterlines, or whatever other crazy, unexpected twists and turns your dream journey takes you on. It's simply the cost of entry. So get as up close and personal as possible with people who are where you want to be and embrace proximity. It's truly the best way to know for sure if you're on the right track.

Talk, Trade, and Takeaway:

1. Who or what do you need to embrace proximity with in order to determine if you are on the right dream track or not?

   _____
   _____
   _____
   _____

2. Make a list of people or organizations who you can reach out to that will help you gain proximity to what you think you want to do.

   _____
   _____
   _____
   _____

Define Stages & Seasons

At twenty-five years of age, teaching music in public school was fun and challenging. What a great combination!

It was year four of marriage with a five-year plan for a baby—and we were expecting! Time to re-evaluate the trades (costs and rewards) in our lives.

Growing music programs require a great deal of extra time and energy outside of regular classroom hours. My school district served many underprivileged families and, unfortunately, had low parental involvement. This called for even greater amounts of work, before and after the school day.

I loved teaching these children. I loved opening their eyes to new opportunity and, even if just for a moment, helping them see beyond their current circumstances to a brighter future. This was my third year with them, so the students seemed like my own children. I had become very attached.

Those three years also taught me what trade was required to have a successful music program. I was happy to make the trade—until that trade involved great amounts of time away from my own child.

The time investment was intense—preparing for musicals and sewing costumes, the early mornings and late hours figuring out how to raise funds for our next concert, class project, or musical instruments. I was happy to make that commitment as a newly married twenty-five-year-old, but not willing to forfeit that amount of time with my son as a new mother.

I wasn't willing to have my newborn child make those sacrifices quite yet. It was important to me to be there to watch him grow, to spend early mornings with him, and not resent my time away. So with a great deal of thought and prayer, and hugs to my beloved students, I took a part-time teaching position at a small private school where I could keep teaching about twenty hours per week. I thought I had it all figured out, but by the end of that year—surprise!—I was pregnant with our second son, Mason.

This was not part of our meticulous five-year plan! Now in a private school setting with better funding and smaller classes it was time for another change. We calculated that it would cost more in childcare than I was making teaching part-time. As my belly grew with child, so my dream grew. I applied for, and accepted, a full-time position teaching elementary music in a thriving district with great parent support.

Honestly, this was the kind of district that music teachers dream of. It was a blessing to take this position and we were excited!

Three years flew by and our eldest son, Aidan was four years old. It was time to enroll him in preschool. I started looking into schedules and realized that if I continued with my same teaching schedule, we'd need to place him in "before and after care." I was the only music instructor at our site so there would be little flexibility in my tight schedule. I realized that I'd probably have to miss the school parties and plays, the musicals, mystery reader days, and of course the teacher interaction I had grown to be such an advocate for.

It was time for another evaluation.

The price tag for this particular teaching dream kept rising and I realized it would be my sons who would do most of the paying. I knew from experience how important parent involvement was in the successful education of a child. I'd become an advocate for parent-teacher collaboration and a building strong student-parent-teacher communication strategies. As driven a gal as I am, I realized that I valued flexibility to match my life's priorities.

Wow, this was going to be a challenge. First, our little family was just getting started and we needed the income. Second, I loved teaching. I loved my students and our school. I didn't really want to leave them, but each night as I rocked my boys to sleep, I knew what I was supposed to do. That constant tug in my gut confirmed it was time.

What would allow me to continue to invest in the lives of students while giving me the flexibility to support my sons' teachers as an involved parent and advocate for education? With tears in my eyes, I turned in my resignation.

But I didn't give up on my dreams of inspiring others through music.

Before the school year ended, I started teaching private voice and piano lessons. Once summer arrived, I taught out of my home one night a week and traveled to students' homes one night a week. With nineteen students, I made just enough income to help meet our family's financial obligations. It looked like time with my family, paired with teaching a couple evenings per week, would be the perfect arrangement.

By August I started looking for office space to teach from. Traveling between homes just wasn't time efficient and when I taught from our home our little toddlers didn't quite understand the importance of a professional teaching environment. My husband and I decided it would be best if I found a little studio. If we brought on another instructor and added about twenty students we could cover our costs.

My dream of teaching began to grow in a different direction than what I thought was the pinnacle of my career.

On November 1, 2011, we opened Abbey Road Academy school of music. I brought on an instructor named, Sam to teach guitar. Our goal was to find him ten students. Before long there was more demand for piano lessons than I could handle, so we brought in another instructor named Kelbert to teach piano. In the evenings when the boys went to sleep, Jon and I would dream aloud about what would and could become of Abbey Road Academy.

"Maybe someday we will have forty students!" I remember saying.

As we continued to grow we added incredible new teachers and offered instruction on more instruments. When we hit forty students, we dreamed of sixty, and at sixty hoped to reach seventy-five. Four years later we had over two-hundred fifty students, twenty teachers, and opened a second location.

I had been so frightened to take the step of faith—to let go of what I thought was my "dream job." But when I did, God truly met me and helped me grow my dream to fit the next season of life.

I share my story for the purpose of encouragement, not comparison. If you are a working parent or teacher who goes in early and stays late to give students the best education, or your clients the best service possible, you are doing work that matters and I applaud you! Every one of the teachers I taught alongside were passionately pursuing the dream and utilizing the gift God had placed inside them.

I share my story because it took me a while to realize that dreams don't often come true all at once. And sometimes dreams change shape. They grow and evolve with the other choices you make and circumstances that take place—in and out of your control. This is good news. If your life takes shape differently than you intended, you don't have to give up on your dream. You may need to adapt and grow your dream to fit your season of life and the people who you care for the most. Taking that small scary step, leads to bigger, better versions of your dream and its impact on others.

Your dream may not look how you thought it would at this stage in life, but it's still there growing inside you, waiting for you to take that next step. It's possible that the time has come to trade one dream for the pursuit of another.

Evaluate and re-evaluate what is most important to you. Dreams are a living thing, and if they aren't growing they are dying.

Dreams grow. You can grow right along with them.

Talk, Trade, and Takeaway:

1. Think back to when you first started pursuing a particular dream. How has that dream changed or grown since you first began pursuing it?

   _____

   _____

   _____

   _____

2. If you've had a dream come to pass, or goal reached, what aspects are as you imagined? Which are different than you expected?

   _____

   _____

   _____

   _____

3. Is it time for you to trade one dream for pursuing another or bigger version of your initial dream? What does that look like for you?

_____

_____

_____

_____

CHAPTER 5:
Define Your Drive

"Iceberg Theory" by Ernest Hemingway says that the deeper meaning of the story shouldn't be evident on the surface, but should shine through implicitly.

It's easy to get wrapped up in chasing our dreams and forget why we started running in the first place. Once we begin to see growth we may forget what is underneath the surface, driving our dream.

It's important we take inventory of what is feeding our drive. Sometimes we start out on a path to prove someone wrong. Sometimes we're in a hurry to get away from where we are so we take any path, whether or not it's the right path or the right time.

What is under the surface is bound to present itself over time, so we might as well dive in and see what we've got working for, or against us.

If you watched the Marvel movie "Black Panther," you know the villain Killmonger has become a fighting and killing machine with a mission to become the King of Wakanda. His drive comes from abandonment and pain, which has grown into anger and bitterness toward the whole world. He is fueled by anger and seeks revenge. He conquers and kills anyone standing in his way.

He is triumphant as a warrior, but is it for the right cause?

In the end, all the triumphs he had over others could not give him what he really needed. Power, control, even becoming King wouldn't heal the hurts of his past. *Bitter roots grow sour fruits.* If anger, resentment, the need to prove something to someone, or approval addiction is feeding your drive, you may not like what grows as a result.

You may even arrive at the destination, only to find the person you set out to prove something to isn't even watching. Don't chase dreams with the mindset that catching them will also catch the ever moving target of approval.

Take time to evaluate the roots of your current dream. Where and why did you begin this journey? Is it what you really want?

As you evaluate what is feeding your drive, let go of past hurts because they only distort your view of what's possible in the future. Choose to forgive. Choose to heal. Let peace, passion, and action feed your drive.

Talk, Trade, and Takeaway:

1. What is feeding your dream drive?

_____

_____

_____

_____

2. Do you need to forgive someone who hurt you in the past in order to grow from a healthier place? List the people and offenses.

_____

_____

_____

_____

3. Since what lies beneath the surface matters, list 3 trades you can make to trade negative drivers for positive, life-giving ones.

_____

_____

_____

_____

Define Your Dream

It's a pretty brave person who is sold out enough to leave everything they know to chase after the unknown. That's what the journey to our dreams promises: the unknown. The excitement, adventure, and adversity of it is thrilling and terrifying at the same time.

Some people have a hard time answering, "What's your dream?" Admittedly, it was easier as a child. There was no resistance or consequence in proclaiming that something incredible would happen in our lives.

Sometimes we are afraid to express what we really want because of the risk of sounding prideful—or worse—never achieving what we've proclaimed. Too often we choose the safe route and respond with something small or reasonable. Sometimes we choose dreams that aren't able to be measured to avoid the feeling of judgement or failure. The problem is, that kind of fearful living isn't fulfilling, nor is it inspiring to others.

Just think, if we had the courage to dream big and proclaim big, wouldn't that give others the permission to do the same?

I'm not suggesting you go on Facebook and proclaim your biggest hopes and wildest dreams to the masses, but I am asking you to say it aloud to yourself.

Let the words resonate. Feel the weight and hope that comes with saying your dream aloud. Confront the fears that rush in.

Write your dream down. See how it looks on paper. Make it real. If it's been a while since you've let yourself dream boldly, here are some questions to get you dreaming.

Talk, Trade, and Takeaway:

1. What do you wake up in the middle of the night thinking about?

   _____

   _____

   _____

   _____

2. What is it that you think you could do, if you dedicated your life to it, that would have the greatest, most lasting impact?

   _____

   _____

   _____

   _____

3. If you had a week free of obligations, how would you spend your time?

   _____

   _____

   _____

   _____

4. What tugs at your heart? What things in life have strong emotional connections for you?

   _____

   _____

   _____

   _____

5. What do you have to say? Who do you need to say it to?

   _____

   _____

   _____

   _____

Action Steps:

1. Write out the characteristics that define your dream. What does it look like? Who is there with you? How does it feel? What attributes of your dream feel most significant to you?

   _____

   _____

   _____

   _____

2. What has to happen to make your dream a reality? Name the next two or three trades you'll need to make in order to progress on your dream journey. Choose with fierce intentionality and determination.

   _____

   _____

   _____

   _____

Optional Additional Creative Action Step:

Create a Picture Board of what you think your Dream might look like. Include the people you would like to share it with and the next 2 or 3 action steps you can see that would help you on your dream journey.

Place your board someplace that you can frequently go to remind yourself of the why behind the sacrifices and work you are putting in to make your dream a reality.

CHAPTER 6:
Decide to Trade Fears for Fuel:

Now that we've learned about the freedom that comes along with trading our fears for faith—it's important we acknowledge that there are some fears that are best confronted and converted into fuel. Let me explain.

My occupation as a music instructor gives me many opportunities to help students face the type of fears that can be traded for faith, or used to fuel their performance. Take stage fright for example. It's an oldie but a goodie, and most of us face it when it's time to make that big presentation at work, sing our first solo, or hit a home run in front of a packed house. Some call it choking under pressure, some call it cracking under pressure. I don't know about you, but I'd like to take a hard pass on choking or cracking!

Recently I had the chance to see not only skill develop before my eyes, but in a matter of weeks, I had the chance to see a student's self-perspective shift and create her dream opportunity.

We had prepared a beautiful vocal duet for our Annual Scholarship Benefit. She had the solo section memorized and came to our home for one final rehearsal the night before the event. We performed for her family and everything went smoothly. Pitch perfect!

The next evening the reward for all the preparation she'd put into this performance was about to come to fruition—in front of hundreds of people. I announced her to our audience and she came to the stage. During the first chorus I noticed her pitch starting to go sharp. By the third chorus she had changed keys altogether and you could tell she was just ready for the song to be over with so she could be put out of her misery.

I knew exactly what had happened. It happens on stages and sports fields and behind podiums all the time. She listened to the negative voices of fear and doubt in her head. We've all been there. Once the negative momentum gets started, it's tough to overcome if you don't have the tools. The next week when we met for our lesson, I had something planned outside of our regular vocal routine.

"Hi, Susie! Today I'd like to invite your mother into the lesson with you."

We gathered in the classroom and I continued. "How did you feel about last week's performance?"

Her head immediately went down, and her mother spoke up. "She was devastated!"

"Alright, that's what I thought. I've seen this a hundred times. I've experienced it myself, and today we are going to conquer it."

Susie looked up and whispered, "Okay."

I asked her to write down all the fears she had about what could go wrong on stage. After a few minutes, she finished her list and I said, "Now, let's talk about what the consequences would be if each of those fears came to pass."

One of her fears was, "What if I mess up the lyrics?" Her answer to this fear was, "Um, I'll just keep going, or make up my own lyrics, I guess."

Next I asked, "How can we give ourselves the best possible chance of avoiding that?"

"Memorize the lyrics and put a cheat sheet on the music stand just in case?" Susie answered.

"Yup, I think that'd work just fine. And if you still flubbed the lyrics, you'd just smile and keep going," I encouraged.

"Oh yeah, I guess you're right," Susie agreed.

It didn't take long before we'd talked through what would happen if each of her fears actually came to pass. Writing down the outcome seemed to ease her fears and helped her realize that even though some of these fears were unlikely to take place, the consequence wasn't life-shattering. She would be okay. She would overcome.

The next public performance was in just a few weeks. During the next lessons, as we rehearsed the song again, I reminded her to turn her fears into fuel.

"Let your fear remind you of how much you love to sing! Instead of letting your fears control you, control your fears. Replace those negative thoughts with positive ones. *I'm gonna rock this performance. I am going to enjoy every minute. I am going to sing with everything in me! If I make a mistake, I'll keep going, and it'll be okay.*"

The date arrived and it was Susie's turn to join me on stage. I gave her a smile and a wink and off we went. Susie sang every note to perfection. I came in with harmony and she held her own like a pro. We finished the performance and I greeted her backstage.

"That felt so good!" she exclaimed. "I am so happy!"

As all teachers do when their student has a light bulb moment, I beamed. "You had it all along. You just changed your self-perspective—you used your fears as fuel."

It's the same for all of us. We have dreams. We might have tuned them out as we listened to our fears tell us about our lack of talent, skill, or opportunity.

We can silence those fears—and replace them with the truth of who we are made to be.

If you have the desire for greatness in a particular area, and you have a natural talent in that area with a determination to build that talent into skill, you can succeed. Take time to calmly confront every fear that comes to mind, and turn it into fuel.

Who would dream of being unlikeable, unsuccessful, insecure, or timid? But that's the recording so many of us play over and over in our minds. Joyce Meyer says, "Where the mind goes, the man follows," and I couldn't agree more.

Talk, Trade, and Takeaway:

1. What practical fears do you face about going "on stage" with your dream?

   _____

   _____

   _____

   _____

2. Earlier we completed a table replacing our fears with faith. Now let's consider if our fears actually take place. Follow it through…

Fear Happens....	Then What?

3. How can I turn my fears into fuel—and in doing so, make fear work for me instead of against me?

   _____

   _____

   _____

   _____

4. When is the next chance for you to face your fears?

   _____

   _____

   _____

   _____

Commit to taking the next step with boldness! You can do it!

Decide to Trade A Poor Self-Image for Truth

Usually we're our own worst enemy when it comes to dreams. Sure, there are dream killers out there, but I'd bet that dream-suicide happens way more often.

It's not that we intend to cut ourselves down or stop ourselves short of success, but our own voice is the one we hear and listen to most. We tend to be our harshest critics and judge ourselves more severely than we would others. Be careful what you think about—but even more protective of what you say about yourself.

Please don't say things like, "Well, I hope I can but I probably won't. I wish I could, but there are so many others more qualified. I'm just not good enough. I've always been this way. It's just my luck. I always get overlooked. I'm insecure. That's the story of my life." Sadly, the more we make these declarations, the more we become a self-fulfilled prophesy—to our own demise.

Poor self-image will hold you back from success in almost every area of life. If you don't have confidence in yourself, you won't go after the relationships you desire, the job promotions, the best opportunities, or open doors—and you certainly won't be proactively leading others.

If we want to live our best lives, we must trade a poor self-image and negative talk for the truth. Are you willing to make that trade?

Some people seem to almost relish self-doubt, but it's not doing anyone any favors. It's important to find strength in the truth of who we are becoming even when the evidence we see confirms the fear that we are falling short. Develop a habit of encouraging and challenging yourself to pick up each day where you left off the day before.

We aren't seeking perfection, we are seeking progress.

Encourage and challenge yourself to trade past shortcomings for small victories on your daily journey. When the voice of self-doubt whispers why you won't succeed, trade those thoughts for reminders of how far you've already come. Remind yourself of why you began this journey, who it has the potential to impact in a positive way, and the progress you've already made.

When it comes to others trying to kill your dream, you may come across a dream killer every now and then. Heck, you may even be related to one. With that in mind, be thoughtful of who you share your dream journey with, and be mindful that you aren't poisoning your own mind with dream killing thoughts. Each time you feel the urge to say or think something negative, trade it for the truth of who you are becoming and where you are going.

It's not enough to try to stop thinking or saying the wrong thing. You must *trade* those thoughts, words, and actions with life-giving ones.

Talk, Trade, and Takeaway:

1. Do you tend to say or think negative things about yourself or your performance? (If so, list some common ones.)

_____

_____

_____

_____

2. When you feel the urge to say something negative what can you think or say instead?

_____

_____

_____

_____

Action Step:

Write it down. Create a personal statement of encouragement to yourself you will have available as you start changing negative thoughts and words into positive ones.

My Personal Encouragement to Myself:

_____

_____

_____

_____

CHAPTER 7:
Decide to Trade Uncertainty for Decisiveness

Every time I go to an ice cream shop I'm that annoying customer who can't make up their mind as to which flavor they'd like. Last time, I just ordered a banana split so I'd only have to narrow it down to three flavors and toppings. (That's not a dietary suggestion by the way, just my love for sweets overtaking my capacity for sound judgement!)

When it comes to uncertainty about your dreams, it's harder to make that call—for a variety of reasons. So if you've made it this far in the book, defined what you think your dream is, but now are finding yourself wavering between the options, read on.

Uncertainty #1: I'm not sure what dream I should chase, so I haven't done anything.

"You can get with this or you can get with that" (Yes, that's a song reference from Black Sheep.) It's like looking into a closet full of clothes and feeling you have nothing to wear. Too many choices can stop us from making a choice.

Should I open an ice cream shop or a puppy rescue?

Should I apply for this job at that incredible company, or start my own business?

If you stay in a constant state of this *or* that—you may lose this *and* that. Let's see if we can gain some clarity.

Remember, each dream involves a *trade*. Instead of focusing on what you think your realized dream will look like, take an inventory of what the day to day operations of that dream would require and whether or not you are willing to make that trade.

Below are some points to ponder—but not for too long; you've been pondering long enough.

a) Do I know the ins and outs of this industry? Am I competent enough to bring excellence and real value? Does this make sense for me? (i.e. *I don't know anything about sound engineering so even though I'm a singer, love music, and teach it, I'm not going to open a recording studio without gaining an education so I can bring value to the customer. Do I really have the desire to put in what would be required to be excellent?*) Be honest about what time, energy, and talent you have to trade and if it's a good fit for you. Don't fall into the "If they can, I can" trap when you haven't evaluated whether or not your unique gifts, talents, personality, work ethic, and investment capacity align with the opportunity.

b) Narrow down your choices to what matches with your personal values. Do you value security over risk and adventure? Do you value family time over profitability? These are important questions to ask yourself to better understand what will make you feel successful. That may not look like someone else's picture of success, and that's okay.

c) Estimate what you think the trade-off for those choices would be: hours per day, financial investment, research, education, and marketing yourself or your product. If it's a position at a company, what are those requirements and benefits? What are their expectations of you? Seeing the choices before you and the trades involved, which do you feel offers you the best chance for success, as *you* define success?

Uncertainty #2: Do I have what it takes?

When you've chosen a direction to take, uncertainty will come from a different angle. It'll whisper things like, "Can I even do this? What if I fail and it costs my pride, my family security, my time, and money? Even if I *can* do it, can I *sustain* it?"

The good news is that pretty much everyone asks themselves the same questions. You aren't alone. The bad news is that even when you are wholeheartedly pursuing your dreams, you'll still ask yourself these questions. But I have more good news. You do not have to listen to those doubts. You can shut them up by answering with positive action. By taking the next step you answer the question, "Am I good enough?" with "Yes, I am good enough—I'm doing it right now!"

It's mind over matter at first—but then it's matter answering a sometimes-critical mind. The action opposes the uncertainty and, over time, replaces it with confidence.

Uncertainty is part of taking on the unknown. It *is* the unknown. That's where dreams live, in the uncertainty, in the unavoidable unknown. Embrace uncertainty—instead of letting it keep you from embracing your destiny.

Author John Maxwell shared a prayer he prays when making a tough decision. "I don't know what's ahead, but You do. I ask that you protect and guide me."

Talk, Trade, and Takeaway:

Take some time to write down the options you are deciding between. Compare and contrast the trade involved and your capacity for success in each direction.

Option #1

Dream:

Trades Required:

Capacity for Success based on what I'm willing to Trade:

Option #2

Dream:

Trades Required:

Capacity for Success based on what I'm willing to Trade:

Decide to Prioritize

It's early in the morning. The sun hasn't risen and the house is quiet. But I'm wide awake, trying to decide between a 6:45AM business networking meeting and getting up in time to make breakfast for my oldest son.

The early morning meeting is a worthy one… with terrific business leaders. Making breakfast for my son is something my husband does a lot of the time… but still, I'm struggling to justify the business networking. I guess it's because I feel like I'm choosing business over family if I'm willing to wake early for a networking meeting but not to scramble eggs and fry bacon.

Maybe you haven't had this type of guilt. But just in case you have, I wanted to address it.

Sure, I attend early morning meetings, as well as evening ones, that take time away from my family. It's certainly part of life to invest time and energy into our careers and business, in order to be successful. It's not about frying bacon or mom guilt. It's not about which is more noble. It's all about keeping a clear perspective on our priorities.

It's easy to feel guilty for getting your nails done rather than working on a contract. It's easy to justify spending time with family even when you know you have deadlines to meet. Make a habit out of choosing the right thing over the comfortable thing.

I don't always get this right, but I'm working at it. Sometimes the pillow is the right choice, sometimes it's not. Sometimes the meeting is a valuable investment, sometimes it is not. You and only you truly know when you are making the right sacrifice.

There is always a trade being made and that's okay. Just be sure you truly believe the trade is a valid one.

Be fully aware of what sacrifice you are really making, and whether or not it is worthy of its reward. In truth, there is zero guarantee of any return on our investment. That's precisely why you want to choose your sacrifices wisely. Don't be fooled into thinking if you make *any* sacrifice, you'll be happy with the reward on the other side.

If I sacrifice too many mornings with my babies in favor of sleep—and only sacrifice sleep for executive board meetings, I may end up with some reward of relationships in our community. But what I want more than that, *and* in combination with that, is for my boys to know how often their mama wakes up thinking about them.

Choose the better sacrifice. It will not be easy but it's simple.

By the way, for my fellow lovers of sleep, there are more studies on the benefit of sleep than I can count, so we don't have to beat ourselves up for that. Just don't get carried away and sleep away precious time that could be spent with the ones you love or pursuing the life you were born to live.

Talk, Trade, and Takeaway:

1. What have you been sacrificing without even realizing it?

   _____

   _____

   _____

   _____

2. What have you prioritized over someone who is longing for your attention?

   _____

   _____

   _____

   _____

3. How can you make the people who are counting on you feel that you're willing to do what it takes to be there for them in the way they need it most?

   _____

   _____

   _____

   _____

Action Steps:

Make eggs and bacon. Ha! Just kidding. Although you can if that sounds good, but what I mean is…

1. Do something today to show the ones you are sacrificing for that they are the reason you wake up in the morning.
2. What sacrifices are you willing to make for your dream? Name them so you know what you are sacrificing and who those sacrifices will impact.
3. What sacrifices are you *not* willing to make?

DREAMTRADER DON'TS

CHAPTER 8:
Don't Allow Dream-Busters

I grew up in a pretty sheltered environment. My parents were wonderful, loving people who lived their lives serving others. Our home was warm and open, and though we didn't have many material possessions we were a happy and generous family.

I was raised in a small church where everybody knew everybody. When it came time to choose a college, I went to my pastor to talk about my future. I had scholarship offers from a two colleges and was hoping to hear back from the third, which was my top choice. As I shared my hopes and dreams with my spiritual leader of eighteen years, his response was, "Well, you can get married, or you can get a degree." He didn't see the point in wanting both, much less any greater hopes for accomplishment in career or community. *What?*

A person I learned from and looked to for spiritual guidance didn't see for me what I saw for myself. He made a point on several occasions, to make me feel small and unworthy. That was his choice to make and not my responsibility to change. I had a strong faith, good parents, and a voice teacher who believed in me and that's all I needed. It was important for me to pursue my education despite what someone else said.

There may be people in your life who put you down. There may be family, longtime friends, or even a spouse who loves you but doesn't currently have the capacity to see beyond where they are in order to encourage you. That's okay, you can still be the one who breaks away.

If you aren't surrounded with inspiring people, and you aren't sure where to find them, *you* are supposed to be the inspiring person. It's work; there will be resistance. However, the reward of helping others find a more fulfilling life is well worth it.

If you aren't surrounded by inspirers yet and want to be the inspirer, there are many resources to add "virtual" mentors into your life. In fact when I first started trying to find mentorship outside of my own personal connections, I started watching leaders on television, beginning with Joyce Meyer. She has an incredible story of overcoming abuse and conquering approval addiction through her relationship with Christ. She shares her story and by doing so, helps thousands of people to do the same. I then sought out other leaders in ministry, business, and education to learn from online and through podcasts...

Some of my favorites:

- My pastor, Craig Groeschel of Life.Church (You can download his Leadership Podcast on iTunes, watch practical messages or purchase his books at *life.Church*)
- Joyce Meyer: Simply search her name online or in your television guide.
- John Maxwell: Just type in his name on Amazon, there's an incredible list of resources.
- Michael Hyatt: This is Your Life Motivational and Practical Life, Leadership, Ministry, and Business Podcast on iTunes.
- Jim Collins: *Good to Great* book is available on Amazon.
- Game Changers with Molly Fletcher: Learn from Incredible Leaders who changed the game in their industry.
- Oprah Winfrey's Master Class Podcast: Learn from Masters in their field.

The important thing is to start and eventually you'll be drawn to like-minded people and they will be drawn to you. When you have a dream, go after it full force and surround yourself with people who are rooting for you, not holding you back.

Talk, Trade, and Takeaway:

1. Who can you intentionally spend more time with to help build your dream?

   _____

   _____

   _____

   _____

2. Who do you need to limit your time with, or eliminate time with altogether, because they aren't building you up?

   _____

   _____

   _____

   _____

Action Steps:

1. Contact at least one person you would like to spend more time with. (See your answer above.)
2. Find one "virtual" mentor to build you up either through broadcast, podcast, church, etc.
3. Support the person, organization, or indirect mentor you chose as you start the habit of being a contributor not just a consumer.

DreamTraders Don't Trade Joy for Approval.

The Voice, American Idol, the X Factor, Who wants to be a Millionaire, YouTube, Instagram, Snapchat, Facebook, Twitter… There are many reasons why these platforms exist, but they all capitalize on one concept very well.

We all desire recognition.

These platforms connect people to an audience that is always watching. With a simple click we are affirmed that others "like" what we posted. With a text to vote, we propel an aspiring star closer to their dream. We love watching American Idol discover incredibly talented people who have been overlooked. Maybe they've had some opportunity but just haven't had a big break in the industry. It's heartwarming to see them be affirmed in what they've been hoping was true but were uncertain of—because the opportunities weren't matching up to their talent.

Social media sites like Facebook and Instagram help connect us to family, friends, and community. But they also answer the questions we are all asking, *Do I matter? Am I beautiful? Do you approve? Do I have something of value to offer?*

We want to be acknowledged—and more than that—we want to be understood for the unique individuals we are. Maybe we like to be mysterious, but we still want folks to *know* we're mysterious, and that makes us unique. We long to be found, to be discovered. We may wait for the knight in shining armor, or the judge on a reality talent show, to uncover what's been overlooked, underestimated, or diminished. Maybe the people in our lives saw our gift, but simply didn't have the means to open the doors for us.

Here's the tragic irony: we know that every human being is searching for validation—how is it we still neglect to give the very thing we know we all desire?

It's like each of us holds the key to the door to someone's dream, while at the same time each of us are searching for the key that someone else is holding. We may want to trade in the key we were given for something better. We may hold it tightly in our fists to keep others from using our special key. It's a rare and beautiful experience when a key-holder chooses to use their key to let another enter through a door that will change their world.

We can all think of "key" people in our life who did open a door—or would not. Here are different types of key-holders.

Key Clincher: "It's my key, I worked for it, and nobody is gonna take it away from me. Get your own!" Insecurity keeps a tight fist. The problem is that when your fist is clenched tight, it isn't open to receive a new key—nor is it open to hold the hands of others and guide them through a door of opportunity.

Key Sharer: "I've got the key to this door of opportunity, it looks like a good fit for you, let me help you through."

Key Creator: "I wasn't given that key, but I know how to create one. It'll take time and effort but it'll be worth it."

Key Duplicator: "I have the key, I will not only share it but teach you, so you share and create an endless stream of open doors."

Recognize any of these people? More importantly, do you see yourself in any of these descriptions?

"Give the very thing you're wishing to get." This statement used to confuse me. *What if I want a million dollars? I can't give that to get that.* It's not a gift of the exact thing you want. Rather a gift of choosing to give to others what they seek, in healthy ways. If you are seeking love, give love to your fellow man, to your family, to your animals, or to your community. If you're seeking a career opportunity, help someone who is just starting out in theirs—make yourself available to answer questions or make introductions.

We all want to be recognized as individuals. Yes, we all share a common humanity, but we are uniquely and wonderfully made. We have different passions, abilities, strengths, desires, and dreams. We don't all want to walk through the same door. We want to be remembered and known for the special traits that make us unique.

Since recognition is what we want, give that away. Seek to see the potential in the people around you. Seek to open doors for others. Thank the key-holders in your life who have opened doors. Don't go through life clinging tightly to the key in your hand.

Don't let your insecurities rule the day. Instead confront your insecurity by exposing it. An insecurity intentionally exposed destroys its power.

Talk, Trade, and Takeaway:

1. What type of key-holder are you currently?
    _____
    _____
    _____
    _____

2. Name some of the key people in your life—the good, bad, and the ugly.
    _____
    _____
    _____
    _____

Action Step:

1. Make a point to call, or send a thank you card to, a positive key-holder in your life—today.
2. List a key that you hold which may have the power to open doors for someone in a life-changing way.
    _____
    _____
3. Who can you intentionally open a door for this week?
    _____
    _____

Don't Wait to be Discovered

Deep down, you may have thought to yourself, *Someday somebody will notice my talent and open a magic door of opportunity for me—and it's going to be amazing!*

As a young adult I had hopes of being discovered. It wasn't until a little later in life I realized *the most important person I needed to discover me, was me.*

It's true that none of us arrive at our destinations without the help and support of others, but don't get stuck waiting on someone else to do the hard work of fulfilling your dreams. At the end of the day, it's our responsibility to make the necessary trades to see progress toward our dreams The best, most generous people will support you on your journey, teach you what they've learned along their way, and encourage you along your way. That said, it's your job to build the skill, competency, and take the risks.

If you're reading this section and thinking, *Dang it, that's me! I've totally been hoping for someone else to discover my awesomeness, instead of focusing on self-discovery and development!* This is going to set you free. Let's do it together.

Release whoever you have been expecting affirmation, approval, or opportunity from. This will free *you* from the disappointment that comes with unmet expectations. It will also free *them* from a responsibility that isn't theirs to carry. Although the beauty and meaning in our lives comes from the relationships we cultivate, it's not anyone else's job to keep you happy, fulfilled, or open every door of opportunity.

You have the power to create your own opportunity—as well as open doors for others. Because I grew up with leaders who did not always build others up, I am passionate about finding the potential in others. I make it part of my mission to help open doors of opportunity for anyone I can. I didn't always have great leaders cheering me on. I truly hope you have that in your life. If you find a few, or even one good friend who will cheer and challenge you, hold on to them.

In return, live your life trying to be that for as many people as you can.

Talk, Trade, and Takeaway:

1. Do you find yourself waiting for someone to discover you? If so, what is one thing you can do today to trade waiting for creating?

   _____

   _____

   _____

   _____

2. Has there been a time in your life you've put an expectation on someone else to open a door and they never did? How can you use that experience to remind yourself to release others (and yourself) from these types of expectations?

   _____

   _____

   _____

   _____

3. Since we all need help on our journeys, who could benefit from your expertise, position, or voice of encouragement?

   _____

   _____

   _____

   _____

Don't be a Blabbermouth

I'm a big talker. If you ask anyone who knows me they'll tell you I could talk to a wall! I've been that way as long as I can remember. I love talking to people about just about anything and everything—politics and religion, the price of oil, the state of public education, or puppies. Let's go, I have an opinion!

I am also a *feeler* so it's easy for me to express my feelings and thoughts with just about anyone. *I mean, surely they'd like to know what I have to say! I have big dreams and everyone should know about them right?* Well, let's think back to the story of Joseph in the Bible.

Regardless of your faith, the story of Joseph is such a good one. If you aren't familiar with it, it's worth reading. There was even a hugely popular Broadway show created around Joseph's dream journey.

Joseph was the youngest of twelve brothers. He was a dreamer and he dreamed big. One of his dreams was that he would be the ruler of the land and his brothers would bow down to him. Now, think of this scene in your own childhood. How would your siblings like it if you told them they'd bow down to you? I haven't tried that one on my sister yet, but I don't think it would go over well.

Joseph didn't think this through. The morning after he had the dream, he told his already-jealous brothers all about it. (This was after he had already shared his other wild dreams which declared him as his father's favorite.) When it comes to sharing your dream, this was the perfect storm of bad timing, jealousy, and poor judgement.

Long story short, (you can read it beginning in Genesis Chapter 37) his brothers beat him up and sold him as a slave to a traveler. Many, many years later, and after a couple prison terms, Joseph ended up ruling Egypt and even reconciled with his brothers.

It's important to be thoughtful of how we make others feel when we choose the time to share our dream. This is a hard one for me. I genuinely love hearing the dreams of people and it's exciting to see them take steps toward it, but everyone doesn't feel that way. If we share our biggest dreams with folks who are struggling to survive, it can come across as cruel. If we share our dreams with folks who are jealous or competitive, it can create unnecessary strife.

There will be enough resistance without adding negativity, hurt feelings, or unsolicited opinions from people who aren't truly invested in your best interests. I struggle with this because I get excited and want to share about what possibilities lie ahead. If you are a talker who is excited about what doors are opening, it takes discipline to keep quiet! Take heart, you aren't minimizing who you are becoming, you aren't minimizing what opportunities might lie ahead, or what dreams you have. You are simply being aware of who you share them with, and the timing. For example, sharing about your big promotion on the day your friend loses their job may not be the best timing, even though it's the right person. On the other hand, if you share your dream of opening your own insurance agency on Main Street with your business competitor before you've signed on the dotted line, you may get into a bidding war for the same property. I'm not saying to be deceitful or sneaky. I'm simply reminding us to think about the *who* and the *when* before we speak.

Your decisions could make your journey much more enjoyable.

Talk, Trade, and Takeaway:

1. Share a time you excitedly shared news with the wrong person, or the right person at the wrong time.

   _____

   _____

   _____

   _____

2. It's fun to celebrate with a trusted friend, who is a safe person for you to share your hopes, dreams, victories, and defeats?

   _____

   _____

   _____

   _____

DREAMTRADERS DEVELOP

CHAPTER 9:

Develop Self-Awareness

Being self-aware doesn't only encompass knowing your limitations, it also means being aware and confident in your strengths.

We've all heard the saying "If you don't believe in yourself, nobody else will." Our perspective of ourselves and the capacity we believe we have to succeed is the most important facet of reaching our dreams. You must see yourself as a success. See yourself as a winner. Envision the finish line and the reward of completing the journey.

The journey is sure to have ups and downs, curves, and even potholes—but when you see yourself at the finish line it motivates you to keep going.

You are enough. You are worthy of success. You are hardworking and diligent.

What you say about yourself in your deepest thoughts will eventually express itself in your life. In the book, *Influence* (Science and Practice) Robert B. Cialdini shares about our human desire to act consistently with the character traits we *think* ourselves to portray. In short, if we see ourselves as someone who cares about education, we will likely support and advocate for education in our community when the opportunity arises. If we see ourselves as a philanthropist, we are likely to support worthy causes to act in accordance with our belief about ourselves. Thus, if we see ourselves as competent, skillful, talented, reliable, hardworking, and dedicated citizens, we are likely to act out in a manner consistent with those self-ideals.

On the other hand if we see ourselves as lazy, indifferent, inconsistent, unreliable, or unmotivated, we are likely to act out in like manner to those perceptions.

Talk, Trade, and Takeaway:

1. List some characteristics you believe about yourself.

   _____

   _____

   _____

   _____

2. List ways you act out consistently with those characteristics.

   _____

   _____

   _____

   _____

3. List some character traits you wish to possess.

   _____

   _____

   _____

   _____

4. List ways you could act out to be consistent with these new traits.

   _____

   _____

   _____

   _____

Develop A System for Saying No

If you want to progress on your dream journey, you'll need to learn to sometimes trade "yes" for "no."

The Clash wrote a song in the 80's called "Should I Stay or Should I Go?" One phrase of the lyrics says, "If I go will there be trouble? If I stay it will be double!"

From a young age, it was hard for me to say no when asked to help fill a need. Having served in a variety of ministry areas—from cleaning toilets to leading worship, children's ministry, and young adult classes—I know there's always a need. You just may not be the one to fill it. The opportunity can either be something that fits your strengths, season, and provides real value, or it can be a time thief that you'll resent.

As our children have gotten older, I've had more and more opportunities to join committees, parent groups, school activities, and the list goes on. One way to keep my motives and time commitments in check is to list out all of the things I am committed to—from PTA committees and our kiddos activities, to School Foundation fundraising, Chamber of Commerce events, and church involvement. I list each one on paper and then write the time commitment required, the number of months or years I plan on continuing to contribute, and my true motives for involvement. (See the chart which follows.) If my motives aren't pure, or in alignment with my purpose and goals, I finish my initial commitment and then choose not to recommit.

Wouldn't it be ironic to join a charitable organization for your own benefit? If you can contribute to a worthy organization that aligns with your core values and stewards contributions and volunteerism well, go for it. Just be sure your motives are in check and your time commitment is clear and manageable.

Talk, Trade, and Takeaway:

1. Share a "Yes" you said out of obligation, that you should have traded for "no." What was the result?

   _____

   _____

   _____

   _____

2. Name a "Yes" you gave with pure motives and what was the result?

   _____

   _____

   _____

   _____

Action Steps:

1. Using the chart below, list the time commitments you have on a weekly basis.
2. Now list the "why" behind each commitment.
3. Create a timeline to let you know when and whether you should recommit or let go.

Organization	Length of Season	Hours per week	Motive: Why I said yes	How I can add value	ROI	Stay or Go?

DreamTraders Develop a Plan

Now that you've discovered your strengths, defined your dream and are a self-aware trading machine (sorry, it rhymed so I went with it), let's develop a plan of action for your success.

There is a time to dream and a time to do. A time to plan and a time to take action. Country artist Toby Keith recorded a song entitled "A Little Less Talk and a Lot More Action." At some point you've got to go beyond talking about your dream and actually take the leap.

We've all had that friend or family member who constantly talks about what they wish they had or what they'd like to do. Maybe we've been that way ourselves. I know I've been guilty of having hopes and dreams—and going on and on about them to those close to me—but not really taking the action steps to make a change. As years go by, the dream stays the same but the movement toward it lays stagnant.

A dream without action is like a car without gasoline. You can look at your car, you can think of all the places it could take you if only you had fuel. You can imagine the possibilities and adventures that lie ahead, but if you don't take the steps to fill up the tank, it's all talk and no action. It's all imagination and no follow through. Stop talking about your dream and take whatever next step you can, small or large, to make it a reality. Your friends and family will thank you for it. As my hubby would say, "Poop or get off the pot!"

Talk, Trade, and Takeaway:

1. What have you been talking about but not acting on?
   _____
   _____
   _____
   _____

2. Write down the foreseeable steps you must take to trade talk for action.

3. Make sure you give yourself a deadline so you can't procrastinate.
   Step:_____Deadline:_____
   Step:_____Deadline:_____
   Step:_____Deadline:_____
   Step:_____Deadline:_____

Develop Persistence

Nothing in this world can take the place of persistence. Talent will not; nothing is more common than unsuccessful men with talent. Genius will not; unrewarded genius is almost a proverb. Education will not: the world is full of educated derelicts. Persistence and determination alone are omnipotent.

—Calvin Coolidge

My husband Jon is one of the most persistent people I know. When he sets a goal, there is no stopping him. Of course my first experience with his persistence was his pursuit of me. (Do you know that he told my old boyfriend that if he ever let go of me he'd never get me back?! How bold!) I think telling him I wouldn't date him because I wanted to focus on getting into the right college just spurred him on even more. Eventually, and thankfully, I gave in to his charms and persistent pursuit.

Everyone likes to be pursued in a positive, appropriate way. Don't we? Whether someone is pursuing you for romance, or recruiting you for a position at their company, it's a good feeling.

However, when we are the ones pursuing, we don't always get what we came for on the first try. It's easy to become discouraged when you get a "no." That's where persistence comes in.

One of my more recent experiences with Jon's persistence was watching him pursue weight loss. If you looked us up on Facebook, you'd see Jon is a handsome son-of-a-gun, but if you looked back several months, you'd notice there used to be a bit more of him. About seventy pounds more.

He didn't just wake up one morning carrying the extra weight. He put it on a pound or three at a time. Sympathy weight during my pregnancies, too many fast food runs during the boys soccer, football, or basketball practices and game seasons, and all the Sunday dinners and celebrations added up over time. And I wasn't much help—Cookies and cupcakes are my love language, so when we weren't eating pizza or cheeseburgers, I was probably baking!

Anyhow, around Christmas time last year Jon got on the scale he had been avoiding, and realized it was time to make a change. From January 1st on, everyone who knows him has seen the transformation. He decided what he wanted, gave himself a deadline, made himself accountable to a couple of good friends, and developed persistence in an area that had been a weakness. Persistence meant trading soda for water, trading pizza for salad, trading chill time for long walks, and trading cheeseburgers for grilled chicken. It wasn't that we simply got into the habit of eating whatever was most convenient.

Convenience usually isn't a key to success.

From January to July, we celebrated Memorial Day, Independence Day, a family ski trip to Colorado, several galas, concerts, and lots of birthday parties—all events that are packed with delicious, decadent food! Jon persisted. He said no to countless cakes, brownies, desserts, cheesy goodness, and ice cold Coca-Colas. He lost seventy pounds in six months and is feeling better than he has in a long time—and looking dang good if I do say so myself!

There are lots of fancy stories about developing persistence. But there are no fancy methods. I wanted to share Jon's story because it's one we can all relate to. Whether it's losing weight, attaining rock-stardom, finishing a degree while you're working and raising a family, saving your marriage, or getting a seat at a particular table of influence—you'll need to develop persistence to see it happen.

You'll have to trade pride for pursuit.

Trade throwing in the towel, for using it to wipe your sweat. Keep going. Trade convenient and average, for difficult but extraordinary.

Talk, Trade, and Takeaway:

1. What will I commit to pursuing with persistence?

_____
_____
_____
_____

2. I want:

_____
_____
_____
_____

3. My deadline:

_____
_____
_____
_____

4. Who can hold me accountable:

_____
_____
_____
_____

5. What convenience will I trade for something more difficult that leads to extraordinary?

_____
_____

CHAPTER 10:

Develop Leadership Skills

"Leaders aren't born, they are made. And they are made just like anything else, through hard work."

—Vince Lombardi

An important element of becoming a DreamTrader is growing your impact and the best way to do that is by growing your influence and leadership skills.

When I think of great leaders, I think of people who act in ways that inspire others toward action. You never know who you might be inspiring, for the good or the bad, without even knowing it. Since we all have influence over someone, and leadership boils down to influence, it's important to take inventory of how we are using the influence we have.

Whether you have a big platform of influence or a small one, it's your responsibility as a DreamTrader, to use that platform wisely. If you want to gain influence in another person's life, or grow your current platform of influence, you must *be* someone and *do* something worth following.

Great leaders earn that title, because they have the ability to inspire others toward action. Maybe their quiet example over time builds their influence. Maybe they influence as they bring excellence consistently through the hills and valleys of life. Maybe they are the best in their field and their excellence rewards them with influence. Or maybe they simply lead a life with integrity and people can't help but be attracted to that. However they gain influence, it has the power to create change in people's lives. That change can look like a shift in mindset, a physical action, or an emotional breakthrough, but it's change all the same.

Who is your favorite leader, and why? One of my favorite leaders is John Maxwell. And, I'm not the only one who agrees, in fact, he's considered the number one leadership expert in America by Inc.com's *Top 50 Leadership and Management Experts.*

So why do so many people look to John for leadership advice? He shares from an experiential perspective rather than only a theoretical one. He's written over 100 books on the subject that inspire his readers to think about the way they think and act in ways that reflect strong character. John must practice what he teaches, because he's grown his business and influence to be one of the most successful, if not the most successful in his field. I love that he shares his advice in a casual, friendly conversational way, that's easy for his readers and listeners to put into action.

My favorite thing about following John Maxwell's leadership, is that it has been consistently sound advice over a long period of time. He continues to learn, and respects his audience enough to bring new thoughts, even though he could probably relax and rest on his past successes. Because he has chosen to lead with consistency and authenticity, he has an incredible following of people—and with that, great influence and impact.

John Maxwell calls himself your friend, but I call him a DreamTrader. He is persistently pursuing his dreams and inspiring and mobilizing others to pursue theirs along the way. This is my favorite combination!

So if you want to be a DreamTrader in any capacity, leadership skills are required. You must develop them to influence others, because with that influence you will duplicate your impact.

Now that we know we need to possess leadership traits, how do we go about evaluating where we fall in the scope of leadership? How do we grow in areas we lack? To put it simply, if leaders are made, what are they made of?

I'm sure I could go on a rant listing hundreds of traits that a good leader possesses, but I'll list seven trades I find to be necessary. Since you've made it this far on your DreamTrader journey, this is a great time to start making trades that will grow your circle of influence.

Trade Perfection for Authenticity: I know some leaders gain short term influence without it, but if a truth surfaces that isn't consistent with the character you portrayed yourself to have, you'll find that your followers quickly leave. Be yourself. Another favorite leader of mine, Craig Groeschel, says "Be yourself. People would rather follow a leader who is always real rather than a leader who is always right."

1. Trade "Solo Spotlight" for "Team Effort" Attitude: Whether it's a politician who pretends to know everything about everything—instead of empowering people who are experts in their fields—or business leaders who are too insecure to empower their team and let their strengths shine, sharing the spotlight builds trust. That trust opens doors to influence those who are choosy about who they follow.

2. Trade Weak Character for Integrity: C.S. Lewis defines integrity as doing the right thing even when no one is watching. If we lack integrity, it will eventually surface, and we will lose the right to lead.

3. Trade Insecurity for Confidence: If you don't possess a sureness of yourself—deep belief that you have what it takes to succeed—others will discern your insecurity and find you hard to follow. It's not a matter of getting everything right or making promises you can't control, but it's being confident enough to know that even if this venture doesn't turn out like you hoped, you have what it takes to succeed.

4. Trade Short Lived Fads for Committed Pursuit: One of the most frustrating things for a follower is a leader who gets excited about a certain mission and as soon as the excitement dies down they abandon it for the next. I'm not talking about changing your method, I'm talking about leaders whose message and mission seem to change with the wind. If you wish to maintain long-term

leadership and influence, find a cause, mission, or purpose you can put down roots with. Commit to see it through.

5. Trade Indecisiveness for Clear Decisions: I shared about this trade earlier in the book when we discussed choosing your dream path. It's an important skill to have for establishing yourself as a leader. *How annoying would it be to follow someone who can't decide on a direction?!*

6. Trade Playing it Safe for Courage: I can't think of a great leader who isn't willing to take risks. It's pretty much the main requirement, even for leaders who have bad intentions. They must be willing to risk loss, rejection, conflict, and failure to pursue something that others are too afraid to pursue. Whether it's taking a political stand, opening the doors to a business with no guarantee of success, standing up for what you believe, representing a cause, being a voice for those who can't speak for themselves, or stepping up when everyone else steps back—leadership requires courage.

7. Trade Talk for Inspiring Action: I believe the best leaders go beyond exciting us with great speeches or entertaining us with talent. The best leaders inspire us to act because they are a living example of what they hope to see in others. When we experience time with a great leader—in person, through spoken word, through written word, by observing their execution in their chosen field, or whatever platform of influence they hold—we know they're leading us when we find ourselves actively *following*. Action is the greatest indicator of influence.

Talk, Trade, and Takeaway:

1. Name a leader who inspires you. What is it they do that inspires you?

   _____

   _____

   _____

   _____

2. Of the trades listed above, which is one you haven't yet made that you will commit to in order to grow in leadership?

   _____

   _____

   _____

   _____

3. If you are a leader, who are your followers? How can you inspire them to action?

   _____

   _____

   _____

   _____

DREAMTRADERS DETERMINE

CHAPTER 11:

Determine the Costs and Make the Necessary Trades

You are fired up! You've got a plan, and are making the trades needed to build your influence while you progress on your dream journey. It's an exciting time, but there are still trades to be made.

The cost of your dream is directly related to the size of your dream. You get what you pay for, or *trade* for!

If you put in the work, make the required trades, and develop the skill to pay the price, you will enjoy the reward of living " the dream." Of course this doesn't mean every little boy who hopes to play in the NBA will achieve that particular goal. What it does mean is as you make the commitment to follow hard after what you are most passionate about, naturally gifted in, and dedicated to bringing your best self to, your life's journey will move you closer to the destiny you were created for.

You may not live the exact dream you started out chasing, (dreams grow, remember?) but the act of pursuing with focus, working with integrity, developing skill, and evaluating your motives along the way is sure to land you in a place that most people would dream about.

For the moment, we'll assume your dream is aligned with your natural strengths and talents. With this in mind, let's count the cost. It's hard to believe, but it seems like many think they can invest minimal time and "magically" reap riches.

Instead of nights out at fun restaurants with friends, you'll likely be pinching pennies to start your business, invest in further education, buy the clothes you need for the interview, work out on the treadmill, write content, design a website, figure taxes, or write your business plan.

Time away from what is comfortable and entertaining is required if you intend to get from here to there—time away from your favorite TV shows and time away from family and friends. Time is a necessary trade that many of us don't want to make.

Everything worth having is going to cost you something. It's just a fact. (Stop clicking on those Facebook ads promising overnight success, okay?)

You won't know the time cost until you're already on the journey, so I suggest tapping into the power of proximity (refer to Chapter 4 Define Proximity as a Good Teacher) and making sure you're on the right track.

Talk, Trade, and Takeaway:

1. What trades have you already made in your dream pursuit?

   _____

   _____

   _____

   _____

2. What have you learned so far by getting into proximity with people who know the 90%-side of your dream?

   _____

   _____

   _____

   _____

3. What cost or trade has caught you by surprise so far on your journey?

   _____

   _____

   _____

   _____

4. Are there any trades you aren't willing to make?

_____

_____

_____

_____

Determine the Financial Trades Required

"Put your money where your mouth is."

When we opened the doors to our business, we used most of our small, but hard-earned, savings. And we had to sign on the dotted line for a commercial lease.

I didn't seek investors or ask for someone else to invest in my dream. There's nothing wrong with doing that, but I believe you shouldn't ask others to do for you what you aren't willing to do for yourself.

The first person to invest in your dream, should be you. That meant tightly-budgeted meal planning and coupon cutting for us. That meant staycations in place of vacations. It meant investing our earnings back into our business and community, instead of spending it all on ourselves.

It isn't the easy trade, but it will help you focus on the core purpose, instead of the lack a money—which can color your motives and hinder your growth and generosity.

Will you put (some of) your money where your dream is?

Talk, Trade, and Takeaway:

1. How much time per day are you trading toward your dream?

    _____
    _____
    _____
    _____

2. How much money have you traded (or are willing to trade) toward your dream?

    _____
    _____
    _____
    _____

Determine Trades Those You Love Most Will Make

Those you love most will help pay for your dream, and I'm not talking about financial costs (although sometimes that may also be the case). There are relationship costs in the pursuit of a dream. It's a reason many of us choose to stop chasing certain dreams.

But the cost can also be an investment that pays rich dividends.

That's why it's so important to communicate often with those closest to you about your dreams, their progress, and how the people closest to you are impacted by them. If your dream is a win for you but a loss for them, it's not the right dream. If your dream is a loss for you but seems like a financial win for them, it's still not the right dream.

I'm blessed to be married to the most wonderful man, Jon. We were high school sweethearts. Fun fact, at sixteen years old he wrote in my school yearbook that I was his dream girl and he would marry me one day. Turns out, he kept his word. We've been married over sixteen years at this point and are looking forward to forever.

Jon and I discuss everything. Since he's a "processor" personality, who likes to take time to think before doing, and I'm a "Let's do this now and think later" type of girl, we balance each other out. I push him toward action and he challenges me to think before taking too many risks. All that to say, before each decision is made to move forward in business, ministry, family, or philanthropic endeavors, we sit down to count the costs together.

Recently, we decided it was time to move one of our music school locations into a new building. It would need a full buildout that would require time and effort beyond our already-tightly-packed work and family schedules. Of course, it would also be a significant financial investment. This wasn't a decision we jumped into haphazardly as it was one that had many known and unknown costs, as well as the chance for great return.

When we finally found the perfect location to build out, we made the decision together. There were long hours, burst pipelines, contractor estimates, and unexpected costs getting from point A to point B—but the important thing was that we were in it together. Jon even played the role of carpenter and built the front desk and coffee bar himself! This would be an impressive contribution for him as part business owner, but even more impressive when you know that he works full-time for Cancer Treatment Centers of America, plays drums for multiple services at LifeChurch each weekend, and helps coach our boys sporting activities. Yes, he's a real-life Superman.

This is just one example of how making the decision together reaped an abundant reward. Include the ones you love as much as you can when you count the costs of fulfilling your dream. That way they know you value their voice. Trade going it solo for sharing your journey.

Four rewards of counting the costs with those who are sure to be paying the bill:

1. Shared ownership of the risks and rewards: you are in it together instead of leaving room for blame or pride.
2. Two heads are better than one. You get the benefit of the other party's strengths. You decrease the chance of blindspots.
3. Clearly communicated understanding of the time, financial, and possible unseen costs required as well as expectations of shared rewards.

4. Bonds of trust are built when you make yourself accountable and vulnerable to another person. Not everyone deserves this level of trust, so be sure this is only shared with an individual who has your best interest at heart.

As you trade going solo for sharing, here are a few pointers to keep the ones you care about most in the loop. Remind them of the Why. Celebrate wins. Put quality time together on your calendar.

Remember: Life > Work (not Work > Life).

Be honest. Don't let guilt keep you from continuing on your journey.

You are more likely to keep a close bond with your loved ones if you involve them in your wins and keep open communication. Set some boundaries together with the understanding that a start-up in any career is going to take time, but you are committed to prioritizing the ones you love with your time and attention. Look for small pockets of time to connect over coffee, a quick lunch, or late dinner. If you have kids, make time for a meal together a few times a week and be sure to do your part with activities.

Including your significant other in the process will keep them from feeling left out and undervalued, plus they'll be part of the celebration as you reach milestones along your dream path.

Remember, your significant other has dreams and goals, too. Catching your dream should not come at the cost of them catching theirs. Work together toward a mutually beneficial end. Dream aloud together, talk openly about how your dreams can align and strengthen one another's momentum.

Protect the relationships that mean the most to you by counting the costs together.

If you have children like we do, you'll need to consider both the costs and benefits that will impact them as you pursue your dreams. I believe the benefits have potential to far outweigh the costs, but it's easy to get so focused on achieving a goal that you lose sight of the reason you set the goal in the first place.

When I left teaching public school and opened our music school, our boys, Aidan and Mason, were toddlers. They didn't know it at the time, but they were the main reason I traded my tenured career with a small but steady paycheck, for the adventurous unknown journey of opening a business. Having the flexibility to be there for so many firsts meant the world to me. Because I made the trade for flexible teaching schedule over 7:00AM–4:00PM public school teaching schedule, I had the chance to attend countless daytime school activities during my boys early childhood developmental years.

Many people didn't understand my choice. "Heather, you have tenure, you have a job that gives you summers off, don't give that up!" Maybe if they were there with me to see Aidan's first class play or Mason's first bike ride, they'd understand.

From first soccer games to learning to read, write, play piano, or simply go for an ice-cream play date, I was there. I got the chance to see Aidan grow from an adventurous daredevil of a kiddo (we were frequent flyers at urgent care with lots of experience in stitches and staples) to an incredible athlete and student with the heart of a lion. I got to see Mason grow from a bright, curious, up-for-anything kiddo into one who has a brilliant mechanical mind paired with a boldness that promises he will see solutions where others see problems—and he's only nine years old!

I could go on and on about all of the experiences we've had together. The point is that there was a cost involved and still are costs involved in owning and running a business. Trades were required, but each memory we've made together due to those trades, makes the cost well worth it.

Right now it's easy to see we made the right decision, but at the start it was a big step of faith, and it was important for me to include my boys in the conversation.

I wrote a letter to each of them, even though they weren't even old enough to read. It shared my hope for a bright future, full of opportunity for them. I wrote about how starting a business would mean that mama would be working some during the evenings for a while, but it would also mean I would have flexibility during the day to be part of their schooling and daytime activities. As our business has grown, I am now able to be home most afternoons a little after their school day ends. I still have the flexibility to be very involved with their schooling and sports.

What I *try* to do very intentionally is explain the "why behind the what." When I do work late hours or attend meetings, I talk with them about the importance of hard work and investing in community. We discuss our civic duties and why it's important to contribute to the way of life we are able to enjoy.

When your loved ones understand *what* you are doing and *why*, they can feel proud. If you don't explain time away, you risk leaving them feeling de-prioritized.

The commitment to communicate will also help you make sure your motives are in line with your values. Constantly evaluate your motives for involvement in organizations, and even work efforts that take time away from your family. Each "yes" comes at a cost. Some are worthy, some are not.

Talk, Trade, and Takeaway:

1. List some ways you involve your significant others in your dream journey.

   _____
   _____
   _____
   _____

2. What dreams does your significant other have and how can you contribute to them?

   _____
   _____
   _____
   _____

3. Make a commitment to communicate the why behind your what with those it will impact most. Who needs to be on that list?

_____

_____

_____

_____

Determine Trades to Make in Friendship

When I decided to go to college I had to say goodbye to some friends I'd known most of my life. When I chose to continue my education in a new city it meant leaving the comforts of home and familiarity of my longest friendships in pursuit of new opportunity.

Some of us kept in touch for a while but over time most of us grew apart. A few years ago I reached out to one of my best childhood friends over Facebook. I thought it would be cool to catch up and see what she'd done with her life over the past fifteen years since graduating high school. I was already planning to be in the city where she lived so I asked her if she'd like to meet up for lunch. The morning we were supposed to meet, I called to confirm our plans and she didn't answer. A couple of hours later she texted that she stayed out late partying and she needed to get to her mom's to pick up her kiddos. Her next texts revealed some of what she partook in the night before and it became evident that our lives had gone in two completely different directions. I don't share this as a jab at her choices, rather as a reminder that it does matter who we choose as companions on our life's journey.

Friends have influence in our lives so it's important to choose them carefully. Many of the folks who start out with you in life will not continue with you as you reach new heights. Most people are with you for a reason and for a season, few will take the full journey with you. Some folks will simply exit on their own. Some you will have to determine to part ways with the understanding that you aren't headed the same direction.

Hurting someone's feelings, or feeling as if you've abandoned someone who you've done life with, isn't easy. There is an emotional and relational cost involved with going where others aren't ready to go on your dream journey. It's a trade many aren't willing to make to see their dreams become reality.

Evaluate your current relationships to see who will wholeheartedly continue with you, and who is likely to hold you back. Choose your traveling companions wisely.

Talk, Trade, and Takeaway:

1. Have you discussed the cost of your dream with your spouse, family, or children as it pertains to them?

   _____

   _____

   _____

   _____

2. As you assess your current relationships, are there any people you need to part ways with?

   _____

   _____

   _____

   _____

3. Name three ways you will commit to prioritizing and involving the people you care most about in your dream journey.

   _____

   _____

   _____

   _____

CHAPTER 12:
Defeat Distractions

Before we discuss areas we need to defeat on our dream journey, let's take a moment to celebrate what you've accomplished so far.

Let's celebrate the fact that you have discovered some of your strengths, defined your dream, traded fears for faith, traded uncertainty for decisiveness and made the decision to include your loved ones in your journey. Wow! Did you know that by simply writing down the answers to the questions up this point in your journey, you are about 42% more likely to achieve your goals and dreams?

According to Dr. Gail Matthews, a psychology professor at the Dominican University in California, we are about 42% more likely to achieve our goals just by writing them down. Goal Band of the UK claims that only three out of every one-hundred adults actually write their goals down on paper.

Now that you know you are in the 3% of folks with a 42% higher rate of actually accomplishing your dreams, let's get laser-focused on taking home what you came for! It's time to make some real headway—and to do this we will need to defeat distractions.

Every year on the day after Thanksgiving, Americans celebrate "Black Friday." It's the day many retailers have the chance to go from loss to a profit. Why? It's the first official day that many start their Christmas shopping. Retailers make a big deal of Black Friday and it's easy to see why. They get a big return on any investment they make to get folks into their stores. Everyone is excited! There are huge lines of shoppers waiting to get the newest, must-have item at 50% off retail for "this hour only, while supplies last!"

Who would fall for such a thing?

Well, every year my sister, mother, and I are there with the other crazies trying to get in on the bargains. How do these stores make money if they offer such deep discounts on popular items? (If we are all in line for a bargain TV, wouldn't we just wait in line, grab our prize, and proudly head out with bargain in hand?)

I'm sure there are ninja-focused shoppers making that single purchase, but most shoppers get distracted and overspend on items they weren't intending to purchase when they walked in the doors.

Walk with me through the doors of Target.

The scene is loud and exciting, Christmas music is playing, you've come with one and only one purchase in mind, a giant-screen television for only $150. You'd be foolish to pass it up!

It's almost like stealing it's so cheap. Who cares if we don't have a wall large enough to hang it, we can always build an addition!

So you head toward the electronics section, but on the way, ever so strategically placed, you notice KitchenAid mixers for $199. *What? Those things are usually $300!* There's gotta be someone who needs one. You could always use it to make Christmas dinner. In the basket it goes. On to the television.

Just then, a vat of plush throw blankets catches your eye. They are only $19! If you wait until next week and realize you need one for Mamaw, you'll pay twice the price. Might as well grab a couple—throw blankets always come in handy. You make it to the TV line but now it's super long. You might as well look around while you wait. It doesn't take long before you snatch up discounted utensils and serving platters, PJs and slippers for the whole family, a bunch of $5 DVDs (just in case you forget someone's kid at Christmas and need an extra gift), and a couple of those huge cans of popcorn—because you never know who might stop by the house—and who doesn't love cheddar popcorn?

You finally make it to the front of the TV line only to be told that they've run out of the discount TVs but they would be happy to ring up the overflowing cart of "deals" you did find! You exit the store excited about all your treasures, rush home to show them to your turkey-filled hubby.

When you pop open the door his first question is, "Did you get the new big screen?"

It's the same way with our dreams.

There will be more opportunities for distraction than we can count. We won't even recognize them as distractions because they're often in the same "department," strategically placed but just off the path to what we really want. We even create our own distractions at times to avoid paying for what we know we really need.

It's easy to spend our time snatching up counterfeit treasures we find along the way. The only problem is, cheddar popcorn goes bad long before a new TV and provides a lot less value.

I must constantly fight the temptation to be distracted, in just about every area of my life. As soon as I set a goal to progress on my dream journey, in floods something or someone urgently needing my attention—or something shiny that seems like more fun than staying on the path. Whether it's the distraction of social media, 26,591 emails in my inbox, chatting with friends, or watching Netflix—I'm guilty!

I've also been guilty of saying "yes" many times in an effort to please someone, all the while knowing I was trading what I valued most for what was easier. Now that's a trade you DreamTraders don't want to make.

Don't trade what you truly want for what is in reach now. This approach even works for dietary trades. Just last night, I was headed straight for a plate of healthy veggies when I was distracted by a big slice of pizza! (For the record, the pizza won.) On any given day of the week I have so many opportunities to get caught up in tasks that *feel* productive in the moment but aren't truly aligned with the bigger goals I so want to attain.

Here's how I'm learning to kick distractions in the tail. I *anticipate* that they'll come my way and plan accordingly. Here is the method to my madness.

Yearly: I set SMART goals. (They are Specific, Measurable, Attainable, Realistic, and Time-Bound.)

For example, here are my categories:

Growth in Relationships (Marriage, Family, Friendships, Mentorships, Strategic)

Growth in Business (Teacher development, student numbers, partnerships, revenue.)

Growth in Faith (daily devotion time, weekly time to think and be still, church, and community contributions.)

Monthly: I track progress by results and evaluate how I'm actually spending my time, not just how I *intend* to spend my time. This is made possible by the weekly schedules I write and the month-at-a-glance markers I put in my calendar. It's a great time to evaluate the "yeses" you've committed to in order to check their alignment with your dream journey goals.

Weekly: Sunday night I write out my objectives and priorities for the week on a week-at-a-glance calendar. So Monday morning I can see my priorities for that day, the time I have allotted for them, and check them off as I go. This helps relieve stress for a driven girl like me. Plus, it helps give me permission to focus on that days' priorities knowing I'll handle the next set of important tasks and strategic meetings for the the days I have them scheduled.

Daily: I look at my priorities, make adjustments for things that come up that are both important and urgent. I also make adjustments for projects that I don't have complete control over the completion of. Maybe I'll have to set reminders to continue follow up to get it pushed through in a timely manner.

Hourly: I give myself, and others, the freedom to adapt to the needs of people. At the end of the day, I value people over productivity. Serving people is the most productive thing you can do, so get your business handled, but don't consider people a distraction. Set boundaries, but plan to take care of the people you value most in your life, as well as allow for the divine distraction of serving others.

Practically speaking, the approach above begins and ends with writing your goals.

You may prefer a different process, but this one has helped me stay very focused and track progress. I don't always get it right, there are times distraction wins, but the idea is to make a habit of trading the instant for the lasting.

You must determine daily to be laser-focused on the priorities of that day, which will lead you to your longer-term dream goals. This year, by golly, you are bringing home the big screen TV!

Talk, Trade, and Takeaway:

1. The best way to defeat distractions is to anticipate them. What distractions do you anticipate will come your way sooner than later?

   _____

   _____

   _____

   _____

Action Step:

On a separate sheet of paper, or calendar of your choice, list the following:

My Yearly Goals:

Monthly Progress and Checkpoints:

Weekly Planned Priorities:

Daily Adaptations and Checklists:

Anticipated Distractions and How I'll handle them:

Defeat Conformity

"Conformity is the jailer of freedom and the enemy of growth."

—President John F. Kennedy

If you want to lead the life of a DreamTrader, you'll have to break out of average and trade conformity for divergence.

When we conform to whatever circumstance we find ourselves in, we give up our right to grow beyond our circumstance. You'll have to get *uncomfortable* to break out of whatever might be holding you back.

Confrontation isn't comfortable but you'll need to confront the circumstance, or choice, that's keeping you from where you want to go.

Change isn't comfortable but it's the only path to new opportunity. Think of this as a trade.

Instead of focusing on what you have to give up to get out of your current state, think of all you have to gain in your new season. Let your imagination run wild with the possibilities that lie ahead for you if you are willing to trade what you know for the world of possibility.

Talk, Trade, and Takeaway:

1. Share a time when you chose not to conform.

   _____

   _____

   _____

   _____

2. How did it feel to leave the unknown and step into change?

   _____

   _____

   _____

   _____

3. How did that choice affect your relationships?

   _____

   _____

   _____

   _____

4. What comfort will you need to trade for opportunity?

   _____

   _____

   _____

   _____

5. Name something positive you can focus on to keep you
   hopeful as you go through the uncomfortable season of
   change.

   _____

   _____

   _____

   _____

CHAPTER 13:

Defeat Frustration

As you start to see progress and growth as you pursue your dream, you are sure to reach what feels like your breaking point. You know, that point where you feel like you have nothing else to give but the job requires more—that point where you need to make a leadership decision quickly that seems to require knowledge beyond your current experience. Or, maybe you feel like you've hit a performance plateau and aren't sure who can help get you to the next level.

This is frustrating. But in order to defeat frustration, you must trade avoiding frustration for embracing it.

I'll go a step further: you must seek out frustration. Yes, really. Here's a practical example.

I teach voice lessons. One of the most common reasons people take lessons is to build their vocal range. That is, they'd like to be able to sing higher notes stronger and louder, or lower notes with more warmth and resonance. The vocal cords produce sound and pitch through vibrations. The faster the vibrations the higher the pitch. To produce a soprano's high C pitch, the vocal cords move at about 1000 vibrations per second! But that's what they're made to do right? Well, most singers will tell you it's not so easy hitting those high notes consistently with clarity, pure tone, and centered pitch without working through some frustration.

Singers have what is commonly referred to as a "break" between their chest and head registers. I won't bore you with the specifics, but it's safe to say that most singers have to work on blending their break to have consistent strength throughout their singing range. It's a challenging part of the human voice that can make great singers stars if they conquer it—and limit performance if they don't.

There are a variety of exercises and vocal techniques that help blend the two registers and make them sound seamless. The results may sound shaky at first. The student may have to correct poor breath control and support habits, or lack of hydration. They may have to consider different music selections than they are accustomed to in order to gain strength where they need it. There are frustrations and failures before they develop confidence.

The frustration is necessary for growth. If you don't go to the point of "I don't know how to do that! This is too hard! I sound like a dying cow!" you can't grow. (Well, maybe not that last statement, but you get the idea.) You must not *avoid* frustration in developing your dream. Big dreams should stretch you, challenge you, and push you to your breaking point. You have the capacity, but you're at your "break."

We all have a breaking point. We all have a rough area that has to be worked through to increase our performance. Don't avoid it, unless you're content to sing in the shower. Embrace the break, embrace the frustration, so that you can shine on whatever stage your dreams take you.

Talk, Trade, and Takeaway:

1. What "break" has you frustrated right now?

   _____

   _____

   _____

   _____

2. What exercises, disciplines, or practice routines do you need to commit to in order to build strength in this area?

   _____

   _____

   _____

   _____

3. Who is a coach or mentor you can bring alongside to hold yourself accountable to grow in this area?

_____

_____

_____

_____

Action Step:

1. Call, email, or text someone you trust about a "Break" (a weak area) that you are committed to work on. Ask them to follow up with you about progress in this area.

Defeat Being Defeated

Those pursuing a dream face times of defeat just like everyone else. The trick is in trading that defeat for stepping into your next opportunity.

I love hearing stories of those who have faced incredible opposition and come through victorious—and even used the struggle to become stronger and more effective leaders. There are so many examples I could share because most everyone who we see as a success, first had the tenacity—and the audacity—to persevere through the hardest of circumstances.

We can go back to Biblical times and reference Moses, Noah, Mary, Peter, Paul, Joseph, or even Jesus Christ himself. We can reference great leaders like Abraham Lincoln who failed many times before he had one of the greatest successes in American history. Consider the founders of our nation and the sacrifices they chose to embrace in order to claim freedom.

Perhaps you're thinking, *That's great, but my dream isn't to free nations or end slavery, I'm just trying to land my dream job.*

Alright, let's bring our search up to date with internationally renowned individuals such as Steve Jobs, or well-known public speakers, ministers, teachers, athletes, political figures, or celebrities. If we want to achieve our dreams we will have to learn how to defeat the feeling of being defeated. We must defeat defeat.

Steve Harvey lived out of his car while he was working for pennies trying to make it as a comedian. Oprah Winfrey grew up in poverty, was sexually abused by multiple family members, gave birth to a child at age fourteen (the child died). Joyce Meyer was sexually and mentally abused for many years by her own father, while her mother didn't speak up or fight for her. Bill Gates' first business miserably failed. Jim Carrey had to drop out of school at the age of fifteen and was homeless for a while, living in a van with his father. Richard Branson has Dyslexia but became a billionaire serial entrepreneur. The list goes on and on. We admire people who overcome major hardships.

As you learn from others while pursuing your dream, I bet you'll be amazed at the adversity they have had to overcome to achieve theirs.

We aspire to be successful when we see others living out their dream, but it's easy to forget the road they traveled to get there. The good news is that with each challenge you have a new opportunity to develop valuable skills. As you face challenges head on and develop the skills to overcome them, you add new skill sets to your tool belt. With a tool belt full of valuable skills and experience, you are able to face, and sometimes even anticipate, incoming adversity with confidence.

Talk, Trade, and Takeaway:

1. What has you feeling defeated?

   _____

   _____

   _____

   _____

2. What opposition are you facing now or anticipate facing as you venture closer to your next destination?

   _____

   _____

   _____

   _____

3. How can you trade defeat for stepping into your next opportunity?

   _____

   _____

   _____

   _____

DreamTraders Defeat the Need for Speed

Growing up, every summer our family would make the twelve hour drive from Oklahoma City, Oklahoma to St. Lucas, Iowa. I know, you're probably jealous of our extravagant vacations.

We actually had a great time visiting the family farm and we looked forward to it each year. My mother is number eleven of my grandparents' fourteen biological children, so it was always a big time with our big family.

The long drive though—"Jeepers!" as my northeastern family members would say. It was a quite a trek in one haul, especially with no mobile devices to keep us entertained. The most common phrase that works ten times out of ten to quickly irritate your parents is, "Are we there yet?" And we used it more times than I can count. We wanted to stop to go to the restroom, stretch, get ice cream, or load up on caffeine and candy at the QuikStop. On a long journey, these sanity breaks can make all the difference.

Trade nonstop for pitstop!

Pit stops on your dream journey are necessary, too. Sometimes it's a quick stop to refresh. Maybe you need a weekend away with your spouse or a day date with your kiddos. Perhaps you just need a day dedicated to personal care (fresh hair and nails perks me up every time!). Maybe for you it's a few hours at the golf course with a couple friends shooting the breeze. Whatever it is for you, don't drive straight through. Take time to enjoy the journey and the people who are traveling with you. Stretch your legs. Breath the fresh air.

Pitstops aren't meant to last forever, so don't get too cozy. Just stop long enough to get the refreshment you need to continue.

Talk, Trade, and Takeaway:

1. When is the last time you took a pitstop to refresh yourself, or someone close to you? How did your perspective change as you got back on the road after taking the time to intentionally pause?

   _____
   _____
   _____
   _____

2. Do you tend to go nonstop until you run out of gas? How can you trade nonstop for a much needed pitstop this week?

   _____
   _____
   _____
   _____

3. Have you ever taken what was supposed to be a quick pitstop and turned it into a staycation? _____
   (If that's you, it's time to get back on the road!)

Defeat Impatience

"Patience is the companion of wisdom."

—Saint Augustine

Since we're on the topic of speed. Let's talk about our tendency to be impatient. I'm guilty. If I'm waiting for more than a couple of minutes for my McAlister's Sweet Tea or Rocket Brothers raspberry Italian soda through the drive-thru, I wonder what's taking so long!

Many of us are accustomed to pretty much getting what we want, when we want it—and it has ruined us when it comes to waiting for things that have real value.

Steve Jobs put it well, "Pixar is seen by a lot of folks as an overnight success, but if you look closely, most overnight successes took a long time."

Adrien Brody said it this way, "My dad told me, "It takes fifteen years to be an overnight success, it took me seventeen and a half years."

You get the point. There really are no overnight successes. Expect to work at your craft every day. Expect to trade your time, energy, talent, money, brain power, creativity, pride, and everything else required to see your dreams come true.

Expect and embrace the time it takes to build something of value. Trade impatience, for a craftsman type quality that only comes with experience and time.

Whether it's an art form, a technology to make daily tasks more efficient, a reputation of integrity or a brand we all learn to trust—it's going to take time to grow into the best version of itself.

Learn to enjoy the grind of small beginnings and the reward of being patient. It's not something I'm great at, I'm usually looking for whatever it is I need to be doing to produce or perform, but I am learning that it's easier to be persistent and patient than to be persistent and impatient.

Since we can't control everything or everyone around us, we might as well settle in and enjoy the ride. Be persistent in your work ethic, but be patient in what you feel entitled to.

Talk, Trade, and Takeaway:

1. Describe a time when your impatience got the best of you.

   _____

   _____

   _____

   _____

2. What do you need to wait patiently for?

   _____

   _____

   _____

   _____

3. When someone has an attitude of entitlement, it leaves a bad taste in everyone's mouth. What have you caught yourself feeling entitled to without putting the work in?

   _____

   _____

   _____

   _____

4. As you trade impatience for quality, what do you envision that quality to look like in your future?

   _____

   _____

   _____

   _____

CHAPTER 14:

DREAMTRADERS DETOUR

DreamTraders trade the known route for embracing the detours that are sure to lead them into the unknown on their dream journey.

I don't know about where you live, but the roads in Tulsa, Oklahoma seem to be in a constant state of construction.

Seriously, I've lived here since 1999 and cannot remember a time when there wasn't some type of road construction on I40. Construction should mean progress toward better roads right? So construction is really a good thing. Regardless, with construction comes detours. Most of us find these detours annoying, as they tend to cost us extra time on our commute. As annoying as a detour can be at the time, we understand why they are necessary. We know that in order for the construction workers to focus on the section of road that's in need of repair, regular traffic must detour their usual route to reach their destination.

How do detours on our dream journey play out? You've taken the time for self-discovery. You've defined your fears and traded them for faith, or used them as fuel and are starting to see progress. You've even developed a plan for reaching your chosen destination and have determined the costs you are willing to pay and trades you are willing to make to live out your dream. Things are starting to really run on all cylinders. You've experienced some success. Your dream destination may even be in sight, when with squinty eyes you notice those familiar orange traffic drums up ahead. (I didn't know they were called that either, I had to look it up.) The orange drums with their reflective white stripes let you know that your carefully planned route will no longer be open. You'll need to take the detour.

My carefully laid plan of teaching public school music, building a reputable program, earning tenure, and settling into a great school district, was detoured when I realized I didn't want to make the time trades away from my kiddos. *Now what?* I had already progressed, I was tenured, I had a plan, a roadmap per se, for building a public school music program. But there wasn't a clear map or set of directions for the detour. I would have to trade the known course for the unknown. I would need to embrace the detour to realize it could turn out to be an incredible on-ramp to a better version of my original dream. I call these divine detours.

What detour has you off your original course? Maybe it was an unexpected layoff or illness. Maybe, like me, you found yourself unwilling to make certain trades anymore. Whether it's a short detour from your plan while you work on an area in need of repair, or a long detour that lands you in different version of your initial destination, it's time to embrace the change and see where it can lead you.

Once I got over the pain of leaving the known, I started to feel energized by the adventure ahead. I've seen this happen in lots of people's dream journeys. They take one path so far, reach a detour, freak out a bit but finally embrace that things are going to be different. Once they are able to embrace the change and enjoy the journey, they start to see new, exciting opportunities they would have missed had they stayed on their initially planned course.

Now instead of a following a carefully charted course to a known destination, I get to live life with a little more adventure and a lot more freedom.

There's nothing wrong with a carefully planned course, just know that life is unpredictable. You'll need to make adjustments as you journey and you may even change the destination. Try to see the opportunity in each detour. What new scenery is there for you to enjoy? Can it turn into an on-ramp that will lead you to something better than you first planned? I believe it can! I believe there are divine detours out there for all of us if we just decide to embrace them.

Talk, Trade, and Takeaway:

1. What detour has you off the planned course? Or is there a known or familiar course, it's time to trade for a better unknown?

   _____

   _____

   _____

   _____

2. Is there an area in need of repair that needs your attention in order to get back on course, or is this a divine detour that has potentially more possibly than your first planned route?

   _____

   _____

   _____

   _____

3. What are your options as you reflect on the journey and where you are now?

   _____

   _____

   _____

   _____

DreamTraders Ask for Directions

So far you have:
1. Discovered who you are as a dreamer and know what you want to achieve.
2. Defined some of the specific elements that drive and motivate you.
3. Developed a plan for laser-focused success.
4. Detoured from original path a bit and are striving to trade familiar for the unknown.

It's time to trade traveling unaware for getting the guidance you need to reach your destination. It's time to ask for directions.

You know where you want to go, you even have a plan to decrease distractions and focus on priorities. Now is the time to ask for guidance. Asking for help from folks who have been where you want to go, or at least have experience in an area you'd like to grow, is a sure way to get there faster. You know what you want and have taken some of the first steps you'll need to take to get there, but why not learn from other's past mistakes and not waste time repeating them yourself?

I still remember my dad using an actual paper map when we traveled as kids. Next came "Mapquest." This was revolutionary. You simply printed off your directions from their website and followed step by step instructions to reach your destination. (Granted, it helped if you had someone reading them to you—otherwise you were looking down at paper directions, or holding the map on the steering wheel trying not to miss your turn.)

Whether you like asking for directions or not, they make life easier and the journey smoother, with the bonus of ending up at your desired destination. Would you take a trip across country with a specific destination in mind without mapping it out first? Maybe you would if you're an adventurer with some time on your hands, but if you want to reach a specific destination and you're on a timeline, clear directions make all the difference.

If friends have traveled there before, we ask for their recommendations on the best lodging and restaurants. We ask for entertainment suggestions and which historical landmarks we should add to our agenda. So why do so many of us neglect to ask for guidance in our most important journey?

We simply think we have to have all the answers when it comes to our dream path. Our pride keeps us from asking for help. We worry that asking for help indicates some deficiency on our part. In short, we're kidding ourselves. Nobody has done anything great without the help of others.

Many of us realize we need help, but don't know who or how to ask.

I have a few key guides in important areas in my life. I call them mentors. My husband and I have been married almost sixteen years, we have marriage mentors who have been together almost forty years. We go to dinner with them, vacation together, and often meet to check in and seek their advice. Since they have twenty more years' experience in marriage and parenting than we do, we can learn a great deal from them.

I have a mommy mentor who has boys who are about five years older than mine. She helps me relax about some of the struggles and hard choices that come with raising boys.

I have three business mentors from whom I seek advice, feedback, and perspective on almost a weekly basis.

We chose people who've been where we wanted to go. I observed their success, authenticity, and strength of character. I didn't look for perfection in every area, I just looked for good people who had strength and experience in an area I wanted to grow. I then approached them and asked if they would consider being my mentor in that area.

When they agreed, I was careful to respect their time. I also committed to be honest, prepared, and to listen to their wise advice. This doesn't mean I disregard my own gut feelings on tough decisions, but it does mean I respect my mentors enough to consider the counsel they give and follow up with them to discuss. Mark Roberts has been my business mentor for five years. It's pretty incredible to see how far we've come since he has been available in this role for me. Debbie and Brett Thomas have been our marriage mentors for over three years and have been a huge blessing to our family. Leslie Lancaster started being a mommy mentor to me about seven years ago, I don't call on her as often as I used to, but she was there during some pretty important decisions that made a big impact on our family.

I didn't always have mentors, at least not direct ones. My parents mentored me, of course, and are still incredible influences in my life in every area. My sister, Heidi, is a constant friend who also mentors me in just about every area.

Regardless of who you have in your circle, you can develop rewarding relationships with mentors in every facet of your dream. Remember there are successful DreamTraders out there who will value the opportunity to mentor you.

How to Choose and Reach Out to a Road Guide (Mentor):

1. Be aware of your surroundings. Who at your job shows constant integrity? Who at your church seems to be successful in their marriage or business? Who at your gym shows incredible consistency and discipline? Who at your child's school seems to be great at building community, or just parenting in general. Write their names, and the area of focus.

Name of Guide	Topic to Focus on with them.

2. Find an appropriate time to ask if they would be willing to mentor you. Be kind. Be humble. Be prepared with questions. Be time considerate-do not ask them for countless hours. Start with a fifteen-minute phone call, and maybe progress to a coffee once every other month.
3. If they say yes, be ready, and follow through. It's your job as the mentee to ask the questions and to follow up on their feedback.

If you find yourself in a place where there aren't possible mentor candidates, there's still hope! Please see the previous section in Chapter [8] where I listed some of my virtual mentors. I've added many mentors to that list who I have learned a great deal from without ever meeting them in person. Start with this strategy and you are sure to find real-life mentors.

Action Step:

Pose the following question to Facebook, Instagram, or to a few close friends:

"What book should I read or podcast do you recommend on the subject of _____?"

Book Title/ Podcast Suggestion	Author	Topic

As a bonus, you'll also learn which of your friends might have some knowledge in an area you want to learn about.

DreamTraders are Accountable

If you haven't already, it's time to create accountability on your dream journey. Here goes...

The name of my dream:

_____

Action Steps:	Deadline:	Whom I'll ask to hold me accountable:

CHAPTER 15:

Trade Interruptions for Adjustments

"I can't change the direction of the wind, but I can adjust my sails to always reach my destination."

—Jimmy Dean

Don't you just hate it when you're deep in sleep, snuggled warm in your bed, and enjoying a sweet dream when suddenly…tap, tap, tap. Or most often in our house, "Ruff, Ruff, Ruff!" our dog, Buddy lets us know it's time for him to go out.

Life tends to shake us out of our "warm and fuzzy" just when we least expect it. These awakenings happen to all of us. Sometimes our health fails us. The unexpected loss of a loved one shakes us. Difficult parenting situations or educational needs of a child catch us unprepared. A hurtful relationship may leave us feeling lonely and broken. Job loss or a major unexpected expense can feel like everything is on hold financially while the rest of the world moves on.

On the other hand, a positive interruption may take you by surprise. Pregnancy, a marriage proposal, a new career opportunity, a loved one getting an opportunity that creates new opportunities for you. It's real. It's life. We get interrupted.

At this point in our journey, my divine detour had lead me to the adventurous on-ramp of opening a school of music. It was exciting times. Abbey Road Academy had just turned four years old and we were celebrating the opening of our second location. We were seeing growth and success. Everyone was excited and we were moving forward full speed ahead! I was trying to balance leading two locations with being an involved mama, wife, music instructor, studio manager, businesswomen, and worship singer who contributed to our community. I thought I was doing okay, most days anyway, until the oil and gas industry crashed. And in Oklahoma, that really hurts.

For the first time we started having students discontinue lessons due to job loss. Yes, right after opening our second location.

That's okay, I thought. *At least we still have this amazing team of teachers. We will bounce back!*

Over the next eight months something even harder took place. After having almost no teacher turnover for four years, Libby, Maggie, Kenzie, Adam, Daniel, Ariel, Whitley, Brice, Josh, and Kamber (Ten of our twenty-two amazing teachers) left the academy—seemingly all at once! Their reasons included marriage, new opportunities for their dreams, spouses' job changes.

How can I survive this? How can we keep our wonderful culture without these important people?

This seemed like too much. In our short four and a half years, this was the hardest eight months in our business. Each person who was leaving had a positive reason, they all left on wonderful terms and gave me plenty of notice. I celebrated with them. This was part of life's journey and part of their path.

But this was also the time I learned the most about why we do what we do.

We aren't just in the business of growing the dreams of our students, but we are in the business of developing the dreams of everyone connected with the Academy. Every one of the teachers who left Abbey Road Academy, left to pursue the next steps in their dream journey! Each invested a great deal in their students, and it was now a new season in their lives. How could I be sad about that? I just hadn't expected all of their next steps to take place within a six month period.

Even with knowing all of that practically, it was very hard—and still is to watch them go because I value them so much. Let's be honest, it's not easy to replace gifted staff.

On top of this, my husband lost both grandmothers, a great aunt, and his father. And I lost an aunt within the same few months. Like the saying goes, "When it rains it pours." Maybe I should have paid more attention to the thunder!

Truthfully, as happy go lucky a person I am, this season shook me. These losses were deeply personal. They hurt. *All at once? This wasn't fair.*

Maybe it wasn't fair, maybe we deserved a time to breathe and heal, but the truth is, life goes on. Time keeps marching and the world keeps turning—even if you pray for it all to stop so you can figure out your next move.

Thankfully we were surrounded by amazing family, church, and a community of friends who were there for our family's losses.

But what did that mean for my dream of running a successful, growing music school that would shape musical minds, open doors of opportunity, and build confidence of students and teachers alike? Would it turn out to be a nightmare? Would we have to close our doors or drastically decrease enrollment because of lack of staff?

Another saying goes, "When one door closes, another one opens." Sometimes if you go too long uninterrupted, you won't even look for new open doors. Likewise, if you stare at the closed door, you won't even see the new doors opening.

It's really easy to get cozy in our day to day routine, especially when we see some success. It's easy to overlook small opportunities to invest in your dream when you're only looking for the big ones. As much as I would have loved for all of the teacher's I mentioned to stay, (and if you are one of them reading this book and you ever want to teach here again, the job is yours!) the experience was a priceless lesson.

You mustn't let what seems (almost certainly) to be an interruption of your dream, stop your pursuit. One person's exit allows for another's entrance. Somcone's new opportunity was once another person's stepping stone on their dream journey.

You've got to trade what feels like a massive interruption, for the chance to reflect on what is driving your dream. That way, the next time your path leads to the unexpected, you are better equipped to handle it.

Some Things I've Learned About the Business of Dreams

With every transition, I learned the importance of having a procedure to handle changes with professionalism and as much care and efficiency possible.

Secondly, I learned that if you treat your employees with respect and love, they'll help find you their replacement! Thirdly, I learned that a company's culture is not created nor dissolved by one individual, instead it is repeated by each and every person on staff.

Live your culture. Verbalize it. Protect and establish it in the daily interactions with one another and your clients. I also learned that there are so many wonderful people we never would have met, had we not stretched outside of our comfort zones. The transitions weren't easy. They took tedious planning. There were long nights and last minute changes. However, we found great people to take over instruction for each and every instructor we said farewell to.

We learned to adapt and put systems in place to ensure our students and culture would be well taken care of. We learned not to place the burden of the future of the company on any individual personality but to hire well and continue to invest in people because the hope isn't for them to stay forever, but for them to learn something and be better for their time with us. Should the time come for them to move on, we hope they'll cherish their time with us and look back on it as a positive step on their journey to their dream.

A Few Things I've Learned on the Personal Side of Things

First, our faith and trust in God and the good plan he has for our life matters. Reading His word, listening to the truth of His faithfulness and reminding ourselves of all the times He has taken something not fun and used it for good. Reflecting on past struggles we've come out of kept our spirits up and our minds at ease.

Secondly, everyone has loss. The loss we experience may seem minor to some who has faced greater tragedies. That's okay. We all have our own struggles and it's important to recognize that everyone has interruptions. Life doesn't hand out free passes to your dreams. So whether you are hurting or in a time of celebration, be aware of the people close to you. It's your honor to help surround them with support and love in whatever season they are in. You'll find that if you are that support for others, they will in turn be there for you.

Lastly, chasing dreams should never come before chasing the people you love and letting them know you care—often. Time is precious—not because of how productive you can be or how much money you can make—but because it's running out on all of us. Use your time wisely. As you chase your dreams, remember to bring your family and friends along for the ride. Not to use them as fuel for your fire, but to make the journey memorable and the dream worth sharing.

Talk, Trade, and Takeaway:

1. Share a time when your plans got interrupted.

   _____
   _____
   _____
   _____

2. What interruptions do you need to handle before you can continue on your journey?

   _____
   _____
   _____
   _____

3. What can you embrace and learn from those interruptions?

   _____
   _____
   _____
   _____

4. Who do you want beside you on your journey for the long haul? How can you treat them like the champion they are and not like an interruption, distraction or burden to carry on your dream journey?

_____

_____

_____

_____

DreamTraders Embrace Change

"May your choices reflect your hopes, not your fears."

—Nelson Mandela

DreamTraders trade holding onto the same, for embracing change.

As I'm writing my first book to share what I've learned thus far in pursuing my dreams and helping build the dreams of those around me, the unexpected happened. I mean, do we ever really expect to get a "Cease and Desist" letter in the mail from Universal Music Group? Um, no.

I absolutely did not expect that but it happened all the same. Thursday, September 21, 2017. Makes me think of the song "September" except for the fact that this wasn't my favorite day to celebrate. I awoke to an email and certified letter from Universal Music Group asking me to stop doing business under the name "Abbey Road Academy" within 10 days.

I'd spent the previous six years putting everything into building that brand in our communities and the hard work was paying off. Finally we had a measure of brand recognition in both communities where we were located. We registered our Trademark in the State of Oklahoma. I had a professional create our own logo and signage. We hadn't stolen or infringed upon anything to my knowledge, but UMG didn't see it that way.

Universal Music Group owns Abbey Road Studio's in the United Kingdom and Abbey Road Institute of California, and they felt that our company could dilute their brand. We were not targeting the same audience or clientele. My background is music education, not recording and sound engineering. We were not distributing music, so why was this happening to our little music school?

My first instinct was to fight for my name. I talked with some local trademark attorneys and all three told me that I could fight, but UMG had much deeper pockets and a much bigger name. It was probable that I would lose a lot of money and time to come to the same result of changing our business name. We might be able to keep the name for doing business in the State of Oklahoma, but if we ever expanded, we would have to keep fighting.

Even knowing this, I had to at least try. I mean, what kind of feisty female business owner would I be if I didn't fight for what I had worked so hard to build?

So I wrote my own rebuttal and got an attorney's approval to send it. Days passed and I heard nothing. The 10 day period (arbitrary as it was) was coming to an end so I called the attorney at UMG and left a message. I wrote a follow up email with options to post disclaimers on our promotional items and website to quench any confusion. Finally I asked if they wouldn't be satisfied with a disclaimer, could we negotiate a realistic timeline to change our name?

We agreed on nine short months for the transition.

I had to change everything and fast! I couldn't even think of our business as anything other than Abbey Road Academy. It's what we'd worked so hard for all these years. I had chosen the name based on a few components when we first started out. Number one, my voice teacher, Karen Smith-Pearson, told me if I ever opened a business to name it with something starting with an "A" so it would be listed at the top of the yellow pages. (I don't know who uses the yellow pages anymore, but her advice stuck with me.) Number two, the building I first wanted was called "Abbey Road Antiques" and was located two doors down from the building we ended up leasing. Since our street was then known as the antiques district, I thought it would be a fun way to add arts with a little tribute to the past.

The third reason we chose the name "Abbey Road Academy" was that my dad loved the Beatles. (One of their most iconic albums was called "Abbey Road" and they recorded several albums in Abbey Road Studios.) When we looked up the name and domain on Google, it wasn't taken. And Abbey Road Studios in London doesn't teach music. Plus they're in London and we were opening in Jenks, Oklahoma, so I figured the local public wouldn't be confused by the name.

Lastly, I thought the name sounded inclusive and welcoming. I knew from the beginning that our school was going to be student-focused, so I wanted our name to reflect that.

With this letter in hand, I had to rethink the "why" behind our name. The list of things that had to be done was overwhelming. And I couldn't just slap on a new name without it having a conviction and meaning behind it.

I took about two weeks to cry and mourn over the loss of our name, and then got to work. (A pity-pit-stop if you will, but a helpful one to process the loss and change.) A glimmer of hope emerged.

We could focus on who we'd *become* instead of how we started out. This meant cherishing our beginnings, but taking a firm hold on who we are now, who we serve, and what we want to be known for. As I prepared for the teachers meeting I prayed to God for wisdom and guidance.

"How can I lead my teachers if I'm not sure myself?"

I figured I'd get more done writing than worrying, so I opened up Google Docs and entitled my talk, "We get to Choose." Composing talking notes helped solidify within me the direction that was best for our school. There's something about seeing concepts in writing that gave me the courage to share my vision for our company's future with the ones who made it possible.

It was time for the meeting. I took time to share the news about the letter from UMG. Then I shared about the fact that when we started out as Abbey Road Academy, it was a fun name with a nod to the past, but Abbey Road is a specific road and not a place for us to stay forever. The teachers, students, families, and communities we served had together created our own song, chosen our own road for student progress. I encouraged our teachers that we get to choose who we are and who we become.

"We, together, create what is only possible when our diverse gifts, backgrounds, and perspectives collide."

Over the past six years, we had gone from a nod, to a specific place in time, to becoming known as a place that helped people toward their dreams. Our song is our own. It's not a replica of anyone else's melody, but a beautiful orchestration that carries the fingerprints of every person who has walked through our doors. We are One Anthem created by the collision of the beautifully unique Anthems of each individual colliding and ringing out in a harmony only made possible by our diverse gifts. We are no longer Abbey Road Academy. We are Anthem Road Academy. We are the Anthem. We Choose the Road. We are Anthem Road Academy."

After I shared my perspective, I asked for their input. I created a "We get to choose" worksheet. It had questions for everyone to answer honestly and anonymously. "Who do we serve?" "What do we look like when you walk through our doors?" "How do you feel about our future?" "How do we make our students and families feel?" "Why do we teach?"

There was a list of open-ended questions with an intent to get at the heart of why we do what we do. " We get to choose, so what name best defines what we do here?"

Reading their responses and hearing their passion and confidence about our future was like having a band of close friends come share the load I had been carrying on my own for the previous weeks.

Everyone agreed that "Anthem" (a spirited song that identifies a cause or group of people) even *better* defined who we were as a music school.

It was our own. It was a name we could take into our future with no strings attached—thoughtfully chosen based on who we had become.

This was a process I never anticipated and I wouldn't wish it on anyone. However, had I not received that letter, I would never have had reason to look at our name or consider changing it to better represent who we were as a business. It was way too much heartache and work to be done without some pretty intense prompting. Having gone through that change, it's made me further evaluate each part of our business. It made me take time to listen to our teachers even more and learn from their perspective. I think it's beautiful how something that started out as a devastating blow to our little company, ended up bringing us even closer together and gave us the opportunity to re-discover who we were.

When we announced the change, we had opportunity to go public and play the victim, but we chose not to do that. We may have not chosen to be blindsided, but we do get to choose our response.

I shared the details with you in hopes that when you are blindsided on your dream journey, you won't be intimidated. You'll take time to grieve over your loss but you won't allow yourself to stay there. You will remember that your joy, your future, your success or lack thereof is not in the hands of anyone but you. You, my dear, get to choose.

Take a deep breath, get your favorite cup of coffee or tea, find some good people to listen, give feedback, and help you gain fresh perspective. Find a quiet place to talk to God—and even more importantly, listen.

It's incredible how some of the hardest things we face can bring out the best in us—if we let it. Remember, we get to choose.

WE GET TO CHOOSE QUESTIONNAIRE

Who are you?

_____

_____

How do you act?

_____

_____

Who do you serve?

_____

_____

Why are you here?

_____

_____

How do you feel about the future?

_____

_____

How do you make others feel?

_____

_____

What sets you apart?

_____

_____

What do you want to be known for?

_____

_____

You get to decide.

_____

_____

Who are We as a Family, Group, or Organization?

_____

_____

What do we have holding us together?

_____

_____

How can we be better?

_____

_____

CHAPTER 16:

DREAMTRADERS DUPLICATE

DreamTraders duplicate because as they progress on their journeys they can't help but engage other travelers who are also pursuing, or hope to pursue, a brighter future.

When we begin to see the world around us as a place to serve, not just be served, we begin to be aware of how much impact our action (or inaction) has on countless others. We are part of a much bigger picture. Why not trade solo success for duplicating success into the lives of others?

How do we do this? How can helping others win, help you expand your influence and impact?

Partnership, community, and collaboration are the best multipliers I know.

Our influence, impact, and effectiveness compound when we merge our strengths, diverse perspectives, and creativity. Let's trade a life that's only focused on reaching *our* destinations with one that will leave a far-reaching legacy. Let's duplicate.

Duplicate by Opening Doors

My mother and father were the first to open doors for me. Mom opened the door to music for us as young children. She was the choir director when we were young, and that door allowed me to begin singing as far back as I can remember. Dad opened doors, too. He was the one who got me listening to, and loving, the sound of classic rock, folk, and blues music. Lake Wobegon wasn't the coolest radio show to most teenagers, but we sure spent a lot of nights listening to the bands they had as guests on the show between Garrison Keillor's storytelling.

Then there was Mrs. Crittenden, who encouraged me to audition for select choral groups, state contests, and solos. It was during those middle school years when I really began to see myself as a singer.

Isn't it cool how a music instructor following her dream path opened the door for me to follow mine? That's what DreamTrading is all about. I wonder how things might have turned out differently had Mrs. Crittenden chosen not to teach middle school vocal music.

Next up to open a door was a high school counselor. I'm sure she wasn't getting standing ovations every time she helped guide a student in the right direction, but she certainly opened a door for me that changed my life. She encouraged me to take voice lessons to prepare for college auditions. Because of that school counselor following her dream path and investing in others along the way, I found Karen Smith-Pearson. Karen was my first and most cherished vocal instructor. She opened a door of opportunity I would never have found on my own. She opened the door that would pay for my college education; I just had to do the work of stepping through it. She prepared me for college auditions; I just had to show up and sing.

After that, countless professors, ministers, school administrators, mentors, and friends opened doors for me. Sometimes intentionally acting out the DreamTrader life (of course they didn't know it would be called that, but they were living it all the same) and sometimes through simply living a life that modeled excellence. I found that even folks who had no intention of opening doors, taught me so much about keeping them closed that I gained a great education from them as well. Don't you just love how that works out?

The point is, DreamTraders open doors. They make the trades required to step through them themselves and they hold the door open so that others can enjoy a life of opportunity too.

Talk, Trade, and Takeaway:

1. Who has opened doors for you? Intentionally? Unintentionally?

   _____

   _____

   _____

   _____

2. Who can you open a door for?

   _____

   _____

   _____

   _____

Duplicate Through Service Compounding Influence and Impact

My husband, Jon's all-time favorite movie is "The Pursuit of Happyness." The main character, Chris Gardner (played by Will Smith) finds himself losing his wife, his apartment, and his job. He's thrown curveball after curveball as he struggles to feed his child and pursue happiness and security.

After losing everything, he finds himself homeless and struggling just to provide the basic necessities for his son. He then learns of, and applies for, an internship that will prepare him to take a test to be a stockbroker. It's an unpaid internship that requires full-time hours and immense study for his exam.

Chris decides to go for it. He's convinced that if he can get through the program and be selected for a position at this firm, his life will forever be changed.

He is invited to participate in the internship program. Since he's competing with others who aren't dealing with the same survival struggles, he needs to do more work in less time. To do so, Chris comes up with a strategy to maximize his time. He takes no breaks. He skips lunch. He doesn't even waste time hanging the phone up between calls. He must be as efficient and effective with his time in order to stay competitive with his co-interns.

He has every disadvantage, but has the only advantage that truly matters: he wants it more, needs it more, and is more determined than anyone else.

The end of the movie shows him passing the test and being offered a career at a prestigious firm.

While pursuing happiness, times can get really tough. It's easier to give up and find some way to live an okay life and make an okay wage, doing something you have little interest in, just to avoid the pain required to really go after something you want.

"Entrepreneurs are people willing to work eighty hours a week, to avoid working forty." says Lori Greiner, entrepreneur, inventor, and panelist on Shark Tank.

Sacrifice is real. The pain and hurt of our pride is real. Risk is real. But the reward is also real, and success will impact more than just ourselves if we have right motives. Chris's moment of happiness didn't just impact his life—it would teach his son so many valuable life lessons about believing in yourself and doing the hard work of chasing after your dreams. It afforded him and his son a better quality of life and more opportunity. And his story inspired millions of people.

Our dream isn't placed inside us for the sole purpose of making us happy. Our own happiness and sense of fulfillment comes when our dream helps others reach theirs.

Maybe you've been eyeing that corner office at a prestigious firm. Perhaps you'd like to be the most sought after speaker in your region. You may want to open a cupcake shop or start a nonprofit. Your dream may be to perform on a big stage or write a book. Whatever it is, answer the "why behind the what" question.

If your dreams come true, who besides yourself will they impact? If the impact is short term and superficial, you might want to re-evaluate your greater purpose and consider answering another "why?" question.

For example, if your current dream is to lose ten pounds to look good in your swimsuit, that's great. Go for it. But answer the deeper question of what other benefits healthy living might have, outside of swimsuit confidence. Your healthy choices could motivate others who are struggling to eat healthy. If you have a spouse or children they might learn better habits from watching you. Your heart health and blood pressure should see improvement and leave you feeling more energized.

However superficial or simple your dream may start out, you can always add deeper meaning to it—transforming it into something that makes a positive impact beyond yourself. If we don't, we can spend our lives chasing a moving target of "happiness." We can fool ourselves into thinking, *When I get that, or be known, or receive approval, or prove them wrong… then I'll be happy. Then I'll relax and invest in others.*

The problem with "when-then" thinking is that the "then" is never enough. So we create a new "when-then" scenario and repeat the cycle.

Why do you want to reach your dream? Who is at the center of it? How will accomplishing your dream add value to the lives of those around you, and beyond? Trade self-focused dream chasing, for pursuing a dream that adds value to others.

Talk, Trade, and Takeaway:

1. What is your why?

   _____
   _____
   _____
   _____

2. When your dream becomes a reality, who will it impact outside of yourself and how?

   _____
   _____
   _____
   _____

DreamTraders Maximize Impact

DreamTraders are combination of TimeTraders, ValueTraders, and Talent Traders. You may mistake a DreamTrader for one of the other traders, or a combination of the three, and you wouldn't necessarily be wrong.

DreamTraders are talented, they are cause-oriented, they care about giving value and being valued in return. What sets them apart is that they look at the big picture of how their dreams collide with the dreams of others. They are more interested in how their dreams being fulfilled will contribute to the fulfillment of those around them and beyond.

If it's our goal to maximize the impact of our dreams, we must do one of two things.

Our first option is to bring other dreamers alongside us and create an organization that multiplies its influence by growing our TalentTraders from individual-based production into a team effort. A second worthy choice is to join, or stay on with, an existing dream team and contribute your valuable talent and skills to make a collaborative impact.

When DreamTraders realize that whether or not we form our own organization, or choose to join a worthy one, we can be active in the creation of dream collisions. We all have the power to maximize the dreams of those around us when our dreams collide.

There's even an added benefit for us with this worldview. Our vision of the possible expands when we choose to look outside of our own interests. Our world gets smaller and opportunity grows bigger.

Instead of looking at the world as "me versus them," we begin to see the world as "we." Instead of looking at everyone around you as competition to fulfilling your dreams, you see how working together pushes everyone closer to seeing their dreams come to life.

It is changing your thought process from, *How can people help me get where I want to go?* to, *How can I help folks attain their goals?*

Do you see the night and day difference? This is so exciting!

If my dream is to have my own thriving business teaching music and inspiring others to follow their dreams, and your dream is to be a singer on the stage, my dream is to help you reach your dream.

Dreams collide. When they do, power, momentum, and fulfillment is multiplied.

Talk, Trade, and Takeaway:

1. How has reaching a personal goal intersected someone else's path in a positive way?

   _____

   _____

   _____

   _____

2. What are some intentional ways your dream can collide and compound with the dreams of others? (Hint: This is where your vision can be multiplied exponentially! So take some time with this question.)

   _____

   _____

   _____

   _____

DreamTraders Collaborate:

Student-Focused. Community Driven. That's the motto of Anthem Road Academy.

It was easy to choose our motto because we are intentional about living those words every day. When I began teaching I reflected long enough to acknowledge the direct collision my university vocal instructor's dream had with my dream. Because she followed her dreams, I was inspired toward my own—and in doing so she gave me the tools and the courage to pursue them.

When I began teaching children I realized the light I could bring to a student's life when I encouraged them to think bigger and to try harder. Only if I took the steps, made the sacrifices, kept my motives in check, and paid the price required for my dream to begin to take shape, could I ignite that process in someone else.

When we bring our best, when we chase after whatever it is that we feel called to, our pursuit of excellence will activate the dreams of those around us.

When we opened our business and began to gain more awareness of what was happening in the business world, education sector, and our community, our eyes also opened to the impact we could have if we decided to partner with other great organizations to do good work. As we joined forces to collaborate with others, we started to see our efforts have impact—even in small ways. Collaboration is really how the *Community Driven* portion of our motto is acted out.

Over the years, we've used collaborative efforts in some pretty cool ways. Inside the walls of our schools, our teachers collaborate on teaching methods, curriculum, and training techniques. We host "lunch and learns" to collaborate on the best ways to serve our students and community. Outside of our walls we collaborate with nonprofit organizations, local businesses, and schools to bring about positive change. Whether it be joining with the US Attorney's office to provide music for the "Stand Up for Crime Victims" event or co-hosting benefits for kids with cancer, we love finding ways to work together to benefit the most people.

We aren't a huge company. We aren't famous or fancy, we simply understand the power of collaboration. We understand that we can do more good together than we can apart.

Action Step:

Write down one intentional partnership you will pursue to a "win-win" outcome.

_____

_____

_____

_____

DreamTraders Share

One of the most famous dream sharers in US history must have been Martin Luther King Jr.. His courage to share his "I have a dream" speech impacted and inspired the entire nation—and ultimately the world.

There is great power in sharing your dream and inspiring others to set out boldly in pursuit of their own. Dreams inspire dreams. And dreamers inspire dreamers.

When you begin to grasp the real impact that your dream can have on others, you can't help but share it. Think about the strength that one speech gave an entire nation. Think about the weight of that dream and the burden it was to share. Think about the importance of giving a public voice to the dream of so many.

You are not alone in your dream. If God has put it inside of you, it's likely someone else has a passion for the same vision.

We live in the era of "sharing." With social media, people share everything from what they wear to what they eat. They share feelings and ideas. When it comes to your dream, the opportunity to connect with like-minded people people is greater than ever before.

The flip-side is that the people vying for our attention on social media is also greater than ever before. Remember the "quality versus quantity" concept and choose wisely how and what you share—and with whom.

Don't let the bumper-to-bumper traffic on social media discourage you. Look for your best avenues to share and go for it! The opportunity to generously inspire is also greater than ever before.

Talk, Trade, and Takeaway:

1. What do you need to share?

   _____

   _____

   _____

   _____

2. Who is your audience?

   _____

   _____

   _____

   _____

Action Step:

Share something related to your dream with your audience today—
something focused on encouraging them!

CHAPTER 17:

DreamTraders Build Dream Teams

I should learn more about sports, because it seems like this would be the perfect time to have a good sports analogy.

My husband spends hours yelling at football or basketball games. He uses sports analogies all the time—talking about getting the ball down the field, not being a ball hog, and such.. Here's my sports analogy, in my best coaching voice:

If you want to win the game, you need the right players on your team.

Simple as the concept is, sometimes it's easier said than done. We may not feel like we have access to all the right people, or we may not realize the access we do have. Sometimes we are afraid to ask. Well, if you haven't yet, it's time to put on your big boy pants or your big girl heels and make a move.

What positions and personalities would be most important for your dream team? This might mean an actual team of people joining forces for a united cause. For others it will mean team of people you can call on for occasional input and inspiration.

There are many ways to assess individual personalities, and the best combinations for team success. "StrengthsFinder 2.0" is a good place to start. Start with knowing your own strengths. Then bring people around you who have strengths in areas that complement your own and lift weak areas in your organization.

For an organization, the most important step is to determine the culture and environment you want and hire character, skill set, and personalities that fit. You can teach systems and methods but if someone has a poor attitude, slacker work ethic, or a divisive personality, they won't be a great team player regardless of their talent.

Personally, I love to interview job candidates. I love hearing about their past experiences, why they want to teach, who their favorite teacher was, or what age they were when they first stepped on stage.

I can tell a lot about a person just by asking a few questions. You can too! Just pay attention to what they say—and don't say. Sometimes what they don't say is more telling than what they do.

We have about thirty teachers teaching at our academies currently and they are all incredible. I can truly say that with confidence. There was an instance where I hired someone based upon their talent and experience when I wasn't quite sure about their character or if they had a team-player mindset. That was a learning experience for me. It meant a lot of developmental conversations, conflict resolution, and time spent trying to manage someone who just wasn't going to play by our cultural and character standards. Of course it ended with me having to let them go.

Take it from me, hire character first and save yourself the heartache of having to manage people who won't fit your vision. Nobody really wants to be managed and it's no fun having to micro-manage people who you can't trust.

So how do you recruit these character-filled, highly-skilled individuals?

We don't wait for them to stroll through the door. We actively recruit our teachers, because high-character, high-performing people usually hang out with other high-character, high-performing people. So when we need more teachers, we all collaborate on who we think would be a good fit instructionally, and who would be a fun person to add to our environment. I value character first, then competency and passion, but I require all three. We can teach the rest of what's needed to thrive as an instructor at our school.

If your dream doesn't require a staff, you'll still want a group of advisors. Use the questions below to guide your recruitment efforts.

Talk, Trade, and Takeaway:

1. What are the top three traits you value in a team member or advisor? (Hint: these traits shape your culture!)

   _____

   _____

   _____

2. What Personalities would be the best additions to your current culture? Or if you're on your own, what personality-type are you most in need of as an advisor? (i.e. An encourager, a "pusher" who will challenge you, a listener, a numbers geek, a comic, an organizer, a questioner, or a thinker.)

   _____

   _____

   _____

   _____

3. Who do you know that fits the desired personality traits you just listed? (Or who might know the perfect addition to your dream team?)

   _____

   _____

   _____

   _____

CHAPTER 18:

DreamTraders Collide

Allan Trimble. If you aren't familiar with Oklahoma football you might not know the name, but if you know high school football, you know that he was the coach of the Jenks high school football program for twenty-two years.

Among many reputable accomplishments, he led the Jenks Trojans to thirteen state titles in twenty seasons of football. In our hometown, Trojan football is the theme of fall. Trimble is known for being a strong, faith-filled leader both on and off the field. A few years ago, Allan was diagnosed with ALS. His diagnosis shook the community who loved him so dearly. Allan of course responded with all the faith, tenacity, and vigor we all admire him for. Over the past couple of decades as Trimble pursued and lived out his dreams of coaching the best high school football team in the state, he simultaneously inspired, challenged, and developed young men to conquer their fears and chase their dreams of becoming star athletes—and more importantly, live a life of integrity that grants a head held high off the field.

Win or lose, he would tell the boys to keep their head up and be proud of bringing their best. This type of leadership is what gave him longevity as a coach and inspires so many to follow his lead.

This is just one portrait of a DreamTrader. If we look closely, we can see tenacious, bold, unrelenting people who are making the required trades every day to see their dreams—and the dreams of others—become reality. DreamTraders are our teachers, coaches, policemen, firefighters, professors, nurses, doctors, engineers, business owners, musicians, mothers, fathers, care-takers, ministers, bus drivers, technology gurus, and the list goes on and on.

I could try to list all the titles of those pursuing their dreams with courage, while intersecting other's paths to culminate in a beautiful composition only made possible by the collaborative efforts of so many.

Our willingness, or refusal, to make the trades required to pursue our dreams, impacts too many to ignore.

Knowledge is power they say, but it's also responsibility. Now that you're on *your* dream journey, bring others alongside you, and show a less experienced traveler the way. Be bold. Be vigilant. Make the trades required knowing we are all counting on you!

Portrait of A DreamTrader, You!

Your Name
_____

Your Role
_____

Who is Counting on You
_____

Who is Impacted by You Becoming a DreamTrader
_____

On My Journey Through DreamTraders,
I **Discovered**:
_____
_____
_____

I **Defined**:
_____
_____
_____

I **Decided**:
_____
_____
_____

I Determined:

_____

_____

_____

I Developed a plan for progress that looks like…

- ❏ _____
- ❏ _____
- ❏ _____
- ❏ _____
- ❏ _____

I am **Defeating:**

_____

_____

_____

I am **Duplicating** the impact and influence of my dream by

_____

_____

_____

_____

_____

I, _____, am a DreamTrader!

Now it's time to do the work of a DreamTrader. I can't wait to hear all about your journey.

Don't go it alone. Connect with other DreamTraders!

- ❏ Email the author at _dreamtradersbook@gmail.com_ to share your journey.
- ❏ Join the Free Facebook DreamTraders Book Club Community.
- ❏ Review the Book on Amazon,
- ❏ Share the Book on social media and invite friends to join you on your Dream Journey.

❏   Subscribe for exclusive invites to DreamTraders Events and Email dream journey tips @ *dreamtradersbook.com*

❏   Schedule Heather to come speak at your business, school, or church. *www.DreamTradersBook.com*

Acknowledgements:

Jon Turner, I just can't say enough about the guy. He's the listening ear during our nightly "walk the dog and talk about our dreams" walks. He's the "You've got this. And even if you don't, who cares?" voice that encourages me to keep going, even when I'm a bit unsure. He's my daily reminder of God's favor and blessing in our lives. Jon, you are an incredible man—but add in the fantastic husband and father you are and it's almost too much to bear (Keep it up anyway. I love you!) Thanks for loving me for me, and not caring whether I sell a thousand books, or three.

Mom and Dad, you're the best. Somehow I've been blessed with the two most generous, kind, and loving parents ever. Your example of constant love for one another, your family, God, and pretty much anyone you meet, is the reason I believe in the good in people—and the love of God. You are woven tightly in every good part of me.

My sister, Heidi, unwavering, protecting, and true—that's you. Thankful, proud to be your little sis, and fellow lover of sweet tea—that's me. Love you. You are the best sister ever.

Mike Loomis, I've never even shook your hand, but your dreams and mine collide. Fun how that works right into the theme of DreamTraders huh?;) I am so very thankful for the care you took in editing my first book. It's a labor of love for me and it meant so much to have someone with your expertise helping mold it into what I hope brings value to each reader. Thank you!

Jeff and Stephanie Anderson, for being incredible neighbors, parents to your kiddos, lovers of Christ, and of course recommending Mike Loomis as my editor!

Anthem Road Academy teachers present and past, you my dears, are living, breathing DreamTraders every single day. You are full of musical talent, creative inspiration, and were chosen for our team because of the heart you have for investing in others. You inspire me, drive me to keep learning, and remind me of why we do what we do—every time I see and hear you. You are simply incredible and I'm thankful for you every single day. Keep doing work that matters. Shine on.

Pastor Tome Dawson, Ronnie Crowe, Mark Roberts, Stacey South, Debbie Thomas, Austin Taylor, and so many others who have had great impact on my life and leadership through your friendship and devotion to serving God, and others, with excellence.

To all my fellow DreamTraders out there, there are far too many of you to name, but I'm inspired by you daily. Keep trading the past for a brighter tomorrow. Keep trading fear for faith. Keep trading later for now. And when you feel stuck, remember, there is always a trade to be made.

Are you a DreamTrader?

Thank you for investing time with me—and for investing in your dream!

How has this book helped you move forward on your journey?

Do you have questions about being a DreamTrader? Interested in more helpful resources?

Are you interested in bringing this message you students or adults in your community?

I'd love to hear from you! Simply contact me at DreamTradersBook.com and subscribe to our DreamTraders Tips and Events.

About Heather Turner

Heather Turner is the founder and owner of Anthem Road Academy, School of Music. Prior to opening Anthem Road Academy, she taught music in both public and private school settings. Heather is co-founder of Women Who Impact. She also loves leading worship on the weekends at LifeChurch, where she, her husband, and children have attended for more than ten years.

As a speaker, Heather brings a message of unbridled possibility, with a real-life perspective. She actively engages her audience with practical, actionable content for easy application to the needs and goals of the listener.

An eternal optimist, she loves finding the potential in others and drawing it out. When she's not teaching, leading her team at Anthem Road, singing, or collaborating on a community project, you can find Heather at her son's football, basketball, or soccer practices and games. Heather lives in Tulsa, Oklahoma with her husband Jon, two sons, Aidan and Mason, and their dog, Buddy.

DreamTradersBook.com

About Anthem Road Academy:

Anthem Road Academy is a school of music specializing in individual and group lessons in Voice, Piano, Guitar, Drums, Bass, Ukulele, Orchestral Strings, Brass, and Theatre. We have locations in Jenks and Bixby, Oklahoma. If you're looking for high-quality, *Student-Focused, Community-Driven Music Instruction*, you can find us at *www.AnthemRoadAcademy.com*.

About DreamTraders Student Curriculum and Circles:

DreamTraders is thrilled to offer the *DreamTraders Student Edition Curriculum* for public school settings, private school settings, homeschool groups, colleges, churches, and enrichment programs.
DreamTraders Curriculum Workbook Elementary-Intermediate Edition (Grades 3-6)
DreamTraders Curriculum Workbook Middle School Edition (Grades 7-9)
DreamTraders Curriculum Workbook HighSchool and College Edition (10th grade through College)
DreamTradersBook.com

DreamTraders Circles: Social group information is available on the website or simply join on Facebook. Handle "DreamTradersBookClub"
DreamTraders Student Edition Workbook Guides information is also available on website.